How to Talk to Anyone

What You Weren´t Taught about Small Talk, Social Skills, and Talking to Anybody About Anything

© Copyright 2023 - All rights reserved.

The content contained within this book may not be reproduced, duplicated, or transmitted without direct written permission from the author or the publisher.

Under no circumstances will any blame or legal responsibility be held against the publisher, or author, for any damages, reparation, or monetary loss due to the information contained within this book, either directly or indirectly.

Legal Notice:

This book is copyright protected. It is only for personal use. You cannot amend, distribute, sell, use, quote, or paraphrase any part of the content within this book without the consent of the author or publisher.

Disclaimer Notice:

Please note the information contained within this document is for educational and entertainment purposes only. All effort has been executed to present accurate, up-to-date, reliable, and complete information. No warranties of any kind are declared or implied. Readers acknowledge that the author is not engaging in the rendering of legal, financial, medical, or professional advice. The content within this book has been derived from various sources. Please consult a licensed professional before attempting any techniques outlined in this book.

By reading this document, the reader agrees that under no circumstances is the author responsible for any losses, direct or indirect, that are incurred as a result of the use of the information contained within this document, including, but not limited to, errors, omissions, or inaccuracies.

Free Bonus from Andy Gardner

Hi!

My name is Andy Gardner, and first off, I want to THANK YOU for reading my book.

Now you have a chance to join my exclusive email list related to human psychology and self-development so you can get the ebook below for free as well as the potential to get more ebooks for free! Simply click the link below to join.

P.S. Remember that it's 100% free to join the list.

Access your free bonuses here:
https://livetolearn.lpages.co/andy-gardner-how-to-talk-to-anyone-paperback

Table of Contents

INTRODUCTION 1
CHAPTER 1: SMALL TALK; THE MOST IMPORTANT SOCIAL SKILL 3
CHAPTER 2: OVERCOME THIS FIRST 13
CHAPTER 3: SMALL TALK TRICKS FOR THE INTROVERT 22
CHAPTER 4: DO: THE BEST SMALL TALK TOPICS 31
CHAPTER 5: DON'T: THE WORST SMALL TALK TOPICS 40
CHAPTER 6: STRIKE UP A CONVERSATION WITH LITERALLY ANYONE 50
CHAPTER 7: 50 FOOLPROOF QUESTIONS TO ASK ANYONE 62
CHAPTER 8: EYE CONTACT AND BODY LANGUAGE HACKS 73
CHAPTER 9: 5 EVERYDAY SECRETS OF SOCIAL SKILLS MASTERY 85
BONUS: SMALL TALK CHECKLIST 94
CONCLUSION 102
HERE'S ANOTHER BOOK BY ANDY GARDNER THAT YOU MIGHT LIKE 104
FREE BONUS FROM ANDY GARDNER 105
REFERENCES 106

Introduction

Do you struggle to communicate with others? Do you become nervous or frightened every time you have to start a conversation with a new person? Do you wish to enhance your communication abilities but are unsure where to begin? If so, don't worry! This book is your secret weapon!

Communicating with others is crucial for survival and is the foundation for establishing and sustaining relationships. With the right communication skills, even a casual encounter with a stranger can blossom into something more meaningful. If you aren't very good at it, don't fret; everyone has space to grow. You can have total control over the situation.

You might wonder: *How do some people do it?* How can they communicate with people without being concerned or anxious? What if you could do the same? All it takes is a little dedication and work on your part.

This book teaches you all you need to know about connecting with people. It serves as your step-by-step guide to overcoming this hurdle, teaching you the art of maintaining solid relationships with others.

The first step is to shift your mentality more *positively*. Negative thinking prevents you from making progress and moving forward. Developing your communication abilities is easier if you recognize and overcome negative ideas linked with social encounters. People can unknowingly establish a range of undesirable behaviors that often impede their social connections. These tendencies must be avoided, whether they are the desire to correct continuously, get sidetracked, or speak over others. Identifying these unhealthy behaviors is simple; you'll learn how to break those unhelpful habits and build better ones with some intentional work and patience. Ultimately, your relationships with other people will improve.

Communication is more than merely the words you say. Your nonverbal cues are just as important. Improving your body language after realizing its significance makes starting a conversation with a stranger less awkward. This book provides a wide range of strategies for striking up conversations with strangers. If you have trouble starting a conversation or making small chats, you can quickly improve that! Moreover, you'll learn about the necessity of being an *active listener,* opening the door to meaningful discussions and connections.

You can't have a productive relationship if you can't communicate. A good relationship is built on open and candid communication.

This book includes straightforward stages, from chatting with a stranger to developing a lasting friendship. It assists you in developing and maintaining meaningful and long-lasting relationships. Follow our practical tips for maintaining constructive discussions and avoiding harmful connections – your social life will take a new direction.

Are you interested in learning more about great communication? Do you want to develop your verbal and interpersonal skills? Do you want to know the key to engaging in conversation with anyone?

There is no better time to learn about excellent communication, develop your verbal and interpersonal skills, and discover the keys to engaging conversations with anyone. You aren't alone, and you *are* capable of accomplishing your goals.

This book leads you through the steps until you've learned everything about communicating with anybody. Are you eager to meet and converse with new people? If so, continue reading.

Chapter 1: Small Talk; The Most Important Social Skill

Whether you're networking, speaking to a potential long-term client, or looking to make a new best friend, small talk is an essential skill to master. While many believe it's a skill you're born with, the truth is it's a skill that *can be learned*. It can be a nerve-wracking experience, but with the right tips and tricks, you'll get through it like a pro.

Learning how to engage with small talk is an important skill to have to break the ice.
https://unsplash.com/photos/erCPgyXNlto

What Is Small Talk?

In his essay *"The Problem of Meaning in Primitive Languages,"* Bronisław Malinowski coined the term "phatic communication" to describe small talk. The ability to conduct this type of conversation is a social skill – often used to establish rapport or get on another person's good side before moving to more substantive matters. Some dictionaries define small talk as a brief, usually meaningless conversation. However, other definitions give it more weight. While some consider small talk an inessential activity that fills silences and avoids awkwardness, others consider it a necessary strategy to engage with people. Think of small talk as a sort of "gateway behavior" that leads you beyond awkward silences or discomfort. It's a way for people to get comfortable with each other and feel more at ease in a conversation. You can see small talk in action everywhere, from in the elevator to the checkout line at the grocery store.

The Importance of Small Talk

Silicon Valley is home to some of the most innovative minds in the world. It's also a place where people are often highly tech-savvy and focused on their careers, but what relevance does it have to small talk? In Silicon Valley, innovation results from a complex web of social interactions. Google's new campus is designed to foster chance encounters between its employees to promote these interactions. The social networking giant, Facebook, has built a mile-long room to house several thousand employees. Their plans for innovation in architecture include creating vast outdoor areas sandwiched between floors, which they hope will lure workers into public spaces and encourage mixing among people of different professions. The new spaces promote small talk, which is a catalyst for innovation.

Research from Harvard Business School shows that chance conversations with your colleagues improve creativity and performance at work. People say that making small talk makes them feel energized and as if their presence is acknowledged.

Small talk has benefits outside the office space, too. Psychologist Elizabeth Dunn found that brief, seemingly inconsequential social interactions with a barista and other customers – like small talk about the weather or exchanging names – can lead to feelings of belonging and increased happiness. Happier feelings were created merely by smiling at, making eye contact with, and briefly talking to the barista while ordering coffee.

Small talk is a powerful tool for creating connections between people, creating the feeling of being known and connected to others, which, in turn, increases happiness.

Here are several benefits of small talking:
- Improves communication skills
- Develops self-confidence
- Aids in meeting potential connections
- It gives you new ideas for conversation topics
- It helps you pass the time more effectively
- Forces you to speak in public situations
- It assists in getting to know other people
- It enables you to find common ground with others
- It gives you a sense of belonging and community

Purposes of Small Talk

Although it seems trivial, small talk serves numerous interpersonal functions, from establishing rapport to negotiating your place in the social hierarchy. It can help you (and those around you) to establish the nature of your relationships, including those new or changing.

Conversation Opener

When two unfamiliar people meet, they often engage in small talk, indicating they are friendly and want some positive interaction.

At a business meeting, it helps people get to know each other's strengths and expertise. Suppose two people are already familiar with each other. In that case, their small talk serves as an introduction to the more serious topics that follow.

Conversation Ender

Abruptly ending a conversation might give the impression that you don't value the other person's thoughts. Using small talk help soften any rejection, express that you appreciate your relationship with someone, and keep the door open for future contact.

Space Filler

Small talk can be a great way to fill awkward silences with something that doesn't require too much thought. If you don't know what to say or are feeling nervous, small talk can help take the edge off a situation. It can also help you avoid getting stuck on one topic for too long.

Harnessing the Power of Small Talk

Small talk isn't only a social lubricant; it's a means of communication. When you practice small talk, you train yourself to speak more confidently in public and develop better communication skills. You learn to express yourself clearly and concisely while maintaining interest in what the other person is saying. You learn to listen more closely and ask questions that will get you the required information. Not only do these skills help you in day-to-day conversation, but they also improve your professional life. If you have a job that involves interacting with customers or clients, being able to make small talk can mean the difference between a good relationship and an excellent one.

In the history of business, many great partnerships and long-lasting relationships have been formed on the initial basis of casual small talk. Ben & Jerry's was started with a chance meeting leading to casual conversation. The business partners discovered they had many things in common; the rest is history. To make small talk pay off, you don't have to be an ice cream mogul. *Show people you're interested in what they say.*

Without Bill Fernandez, Apple products, such as iPhones, Macbooks, and more, wouldn't exist. Fernandez was a mutual friend of Steve Jobs and Wozniak, and both attended the same junior high school. Jobs and Wozniak first met when introduced by Fernandez. Fernandez had seen Wozniak outside washing his car, so he brought Jobs to meet him – and the two immediately hit it off. They talked about technology and electronics and eventually decided to work together on a project. The result was Apple Computer, Inc., which became the world-renowned company everyone knows today.

If it weren't for small talk, numerous start-ups and companies wouldn't exist. The next time you're in the mood for small talk, think of Steve Jobs, Wozniak, and the other entrepreneurs who owe their success to casual conversation.

Practicing small talk can be daunting if you don't know where to start. The following are the main principles of small talk to help you get started.

Show a Genuine Interest

Conversation is an *art form*. If you want to master it, you have to eliminate the notion that small talk doesn't matter – because it does.

When you meet people for the first time, your conversations are vehicles to improve your communication skills. So, the next time you feel anxious about starting a conversation with someone new, approach it *excitedly* instead. You can't just go through the motions, asking the same questions and waiting for an answer. You have to show a genuine interest in what the other person is saying by asking questions requiring more than one-word answers. For example, instead of asking someone, "What do you do?" ask, "How did you get into your line of work?" If you want to truly connect with someone, ask them about something they're passionate about and listen closely as they answer.

Conversation is an art form.
https://unsplash.com/photos/kFEb8yigiuQ

Put Away Your Phone

Making eye contact with the person you're talking to is essential. It's easy to look down at your phone or glance around the room while someone is talking, but this can signal you're not interested in what they are saying. Making eye contact lets them know you're giving them your full attention, which helps them feel more comfortable around you, and they will open up even more.

It's easy to pull out your phone and check your messages during a conversation, but avoid doing this unless it's an emergency. Ask permission first if you need to text or check social media while talking to someone. If they say no, don't do it. The person will feel ignored, and it could damage your potential relationship.

Don't Be Afraid To Talk About Yourself

When practicing small talk, it can be challenging to chime in with someone else's story or conversation. You might feel you're interrupting, or your contribution isn't valuable enough to warrant a response. However, don't worry. It's okay to talk about yourself. As long as you're not being self-centered or rude, people will easily relate to your words.

Be prepared to share information about yourself, but avoid giving short, closed responses. Instead of responding with a simple yes or no, use your response to provide additional details. This way, the other person will have more material to work from and continue talking without feeling like they're interrogating you.

For example:

Question: "How have you been? What's going on in your life?"

Short response: "I'm good. I just finished my semester."

Better response: "I'm doing well. I'm getting ready for my trip to England, which will be my first time visiting that part of the world. I look forward to drinking some real English tea."

Instead of bringing the conversation to an abrupt stop, you've given the other person something to work with and kept the conversation going.

Question: "How's work?"

Short response: "It's busy."

Better response: "I have a lot of projects going on. However, I'm ready for a break. We're planning on taking some time off over the holidays. What about you?"

By asking a question, you've turned the conversation back to the other person and allowed them to talk about themselves. You can't do this with a one-word answer like "Fine."

Talking about yourself acts as an excellent catalyst to keep the conversation going. It's essential to be aware of how much you say about yourself. People often talk about themselves for the sake of talking about themselves, making them seem self-absorbed or narcissistic. This is a turnoff for most people. Being aware of what you're saying helps you keep this from happening.

Ask Open-Ended Questions

Open-ended questions can't be answered with a simple yes or no. They require more than one-word answers and encourage people to talk about themselves. They give you more information about what's happening in people's lives and help you better understand them as individuals. Open-ended small talk questions encourage the person to open up and share their ideas, feelings, or experiences.

You can ask open-ended questions in various ways; ask them about their life, job, or personal interests. Or ask what they think about something happening in the news or even something more lighthearted, like their weekend. For example, you could ask, "What do you think about the new Facebook update?" or "Have you heard there's a new Star Wars movie coming out in December?"

However, closed-ended or short-ended questions are the opposite. They're usually short and to the point. They can be a great way to get someone's attention or get them talking about something they enjoy, but they don't usually give you much information about the person as an individual. Open-ended questions allow you to find common ground, and once you have something to work with, ask short-ended questions to deepen the conversation.

For example:

You: "What are your hobbies?"

Them: "I like playing video games, reading, and hiking."

You: "What's your favorite book?"

Them: "I love Harry Potter."

You: "Yes. I've read all the books, too. Have you seen the movies?"

It is a great way to take the conversation in any direction. You could talk about your favorite characters, how JK Rowling inspired you, or how many times you've seen each movie. Sometimes short-ended questions don't work as well as open-ended ones, so it's important to know the difference. If someone tells you they have a new puppy and wants to know what dog food it should eat, asking them if it poops on the carpet won't get you very far. Instead, ask them what their favorite dog breed is or if they have other pets. There are no rules when making conversation with strangers. Remember, the person you're talking to wants to have a good time, too. If they say something interesting, ask them more about it.

Practice Active Listening

Keeping the conversation's momentum can be challenging if you are not an active listener. When another person is speaking, *pay attention*, as this will show them you care about what they are saying. You can do this by nodding, smiling, and making eye contact throughout the conversation. By actively listening, you track where the other person is going with their story, making it easier for them to continue talking.

Engagement is key to a good conversation, and active listening is a great way to show you are engaged. In addition, by actively listening, you can pick up on cues the other person might drop. It is an integral part of the conversation because it helps you understand what the other person likes and dislikes; it also makes it easier for them to speak with someone who shares their interests. The following tips will help you become a better active listener:

1. Never interrupt anyone while they are talking, and don't prepare your response until the person has finished speaking.
2. Don't offer unsolicited advice, suggestions, or solutions.
3. Pay attention to a speaker's nonverbal cues, such as tone of voice, facial expression, and body language, to more accurately determine their words' meaning.
4. Avoid being distracted by your thoughts or concerns. Don't think about what you will say in response while the other person is speaking; instead, focus on what they are saying.
5. Be willing to accept new ideas and look past your biases.
6. Ask questions to show you are listening.
7. Repeat what the person said in your words to confirm you understand them correctly.

Show Enthusiasm

Enthusiasm is an effective way to show you are listening and engaged in the conversation. It can be as simple as nodding your head or smiling when someone says something important to them, like *"I really love my job"* or *"My family is what makes me happiest in life."*

Enthusiasm isn't limited to your verbal responses. It can be expressed through your body language. For example, if someone is telling you about their vacation to Hawaii, lean forward and slightly nod while they speak, showing you are interested in what they are saying and want to hear more. Also, use your facial expressions to show you're listening; a smile or slight laugh at the right moment can help keep the conversation going smoothly.

Avoid non-verbal cues that might signal disinterest, like rolling your eyes or folding your arms. If you find it difficult to be enthusiastic about what someone is saying, focus on the facts and skip over your initial reactions. You can shift the focus of the conversation by asking questions about what they said or commenting on how their story relates to something else.

Benefits of Small Talk

It Helps You Relax

When you're in an unfamiliar situation, such as meeting new people or speaking in public, it's normal to feel nervous. Small talk can relieve some of those nerves by giving you something familiar to do.

It Trains You for Bigger Conversations

Making small talk trains your brain to hold conversations with strangers, preparing you for more meaningful discussions later on down the road (making those awkward first dates easier).

It Gets You Out of Your Head

Talking to someone else forces you to concentrate on what they're saying instead of thinking about your problems. It can help you get over an emotional hangover from something that happened earlier in the day or takes your mind off things for a while.

It Makes You More Likable

People like to interact with those who say hello, ask questions, and make them feel good about themselves. Make an effort to connect with others by making eye contact and smiling when they walk by. These simple gestures can go a long way toward making people feel you're interested in them as individuals.

It Makes You a Better Listener

Being interested in what someone else says makes them feel good and helps them learn something new. One thing that can help you succeed in life is listening well and understanding another person's point of view.

It Makes You More Memorable

Being interested in other people and what they say is a great way to make a good impression. People often remember those interested in what they say. So, you can make a lasting impression by asking questions and actively listening rather than simply waiting for your turn to talk.

It Helps You Understand Others' Points of View

Listening closely to someone else's perspective is a great way to learn about what makes them unique and how they see the world. Taking the time to truly listen and consider another person's point of view helps you better understand where they are coming from. It can be especially helpful when working with people from other cultures or backgrounds with different values than yours.

It Shows You Care About Others

Listening is a great way to show people you care about their feelings and opinions. When you genuinely listen to someone, it demonstrates you value what they say and are interested in hearing more. It can strengthen your relationships with others and create a more positive environment.

It Can Improve Your Relationships with Others

When you listen, it helps you develop stronger relationships with the people around you. People feel valued and respected when they know someone truly listens to them. It creates an environment where everyone feels comfortable expressing their feelings, thoughts, and ideas.

Engaging in small talk has many advantages, from gaining critical social skills to becoming a leader with great business opportunities. Hone your small talk skills and discover new confidence in all aspects of life.

Chapter 2: Overcome THIS First

Many people struggle with small talk. It can feel awkward to start a conversation with someone or discuss the weather with a complete stranger. Introverts and people with social anxiety, poor social skills, and low self-esteem can find small talk difficult and sometimes *overwhelming*. However, you can use proven techniques and tricks to overcome the fear and anxiety of small talk.

Social anxiety is a real problem that can keep you from forming healthy relationships.
https://unsplash.com/photos/rXrMy7mXUEs

Mental Health Disclaimer: Some of these struggles require medical attention from a medical health professional. Talk to a therapist if you cannot manage your anxiety or other issues.

Social Anxiety

Social anxiety disorder or social phobia is an overwhelming discomfort, nervousness, or fear of social situations. It usually starts at a young age and can impact social interactions throughout your life. Some people confuse shyness with social anxiety, but the latter is more severe. If you experience panic attacks, sweats, sickness, blushing, embarrassment, stiffness, avoid social situations, avoid eye contact, dread criticism, feel self-conscious, or worry about making small talk, you probably have social anxiety.

For every problem, there is a solution. You can manage your social anxiety with a few proven techniques.

Change Your Attitude

This sounds easier said than done but changing your thoughts and attitude are effective methods to manage social anxiety. Thoughts like "I am socially awkward" or "I am boring" keep you from approaching others and starting a conversation. Understand that these thoughts aren't helpful; your mind is playing tricks on you by presenting negative and distorted ideas about yourself. Be kinder to yourself, exercise self-compassion, and change your thoughts to more positive and realistic ones. Tell yourself, "I am an interesting and friendly person. On more than one occasion, I have noticed that others enjoy my company and conversational skills." Or, "Most people are focused on what I am saying, and they barely notice my anxiety. No one will care or judge me for feeling anxious. Those who judge others for their social anxiety are the ones with the problem. Anyone can experience social anxiety."

Avoid Temporary Solutions

A friend calls to invite you to their birthday party. However, you don't want to endure the awkwardness of small talk, so you avoid going. Avoiding social gatherings isn't going to fix your anxiety. It is a temporary solution because you can't avoid socialization forever. Meeting people and engaging in small talk allows you to practice conversation starters, develop social skills, and gain confidence. The more you interact with others and let the conversation flow naturally, the easier it is to quiet these negative thoughts.

There are two types of avoidance. The first is overt avoidance, which is steering clear of situations that make you uncomfortable, like starting a conversation with someone or attending a fun gathering or activity. The second is covert avoidance, which is shying away from expressing your opinion in front of others, cutting a conversation short, or not speaking much about yourself. There are also physical behaviors related to covert avoidance, like folding your arms, not making eye contact, looking at your phone, and speaking in a low voice. People with social anxiety resort to this behavior, consciously or subconsciously, to remain in the background and avoid attention.

The first thing to do is stop avoiding; simply do the opposite of whatever your anxiety is telling you. Take small steps and gradually get out of your comfort zone. When talking to someone, don't get lost in your negative thoughts. Instead, focus on the conversation and the person you are talking to. Don't rehearse the conversation beforehand, be yourself and speak your mind. Actively listen to what the person is saying and engage in the conversation by asking questions or responding. Don't say what they want to hear or echo their sentiments, but express your own thoughts.

For instance, you are discussing the weather with someone while waiting at the doctor's office. They tell you they don't like the summer and prefer the cold weather. Don't just agree with them. If you aren't a fan of winter, smile and say, "I am a summer person." This admission can invite a conversation where you chat about your favorite seasonal activities. If there is a gap in the conversation, change the subject.

You probably respond with short statements during a conversation because you are afraid others will judge you if you express yourself freely. Make it a rule always to *expand your answers*. It is new territory for you and requires more effort, but it will keep the conversation flowing.

For instance, someone asks you about your day. Instead of just saying "good," give them more details. Say, "I am good, but I have worked so hard this week, I can't wait for the weekend. I am going to binge-watch Wednesday and maybe read a book." You have now introduced a few new topics to the conversation, like work, a TV show, and a book. This will invite the other person to ask you more questions so you can get to know each other better and connect. You will naturally feel anxious at first, but in time, you will notice that others enjoy your company and you are a good conversationalist.

Letting go of these temporary solutions isn't easy and can – at least initially – increase your anxiety. Start with a few minor changes, and don't overwhelm yourself. In time you will feel more at ease, especially when you find it easier to start a conversation with people and engage with them.

Balance the Conversation

Avoid turning a conversation into an interview by asking questions to shift the attention away from yourself. There should be a balance in every conversation where both parties can talk, listen, and know each other better. Set a goal to say as much about yourself as the other person does. Ask them about themselves, but also give them space to ask you questions so you can be a part of the conversation. Remember, communication goes both ways.

Breathe

Take a few deep breaths before social interactions. Breathing can soothe your anxiety by slowing your heart rate and calming your nerves, while stress makes you focus on what can go wrong and question yourself and your abilities. When you breathe, you are mindful of the present moment and focus on the conversation. If you become nervous during a conversation or when someone asks you a question, take a moment to breathe, as it allows you to refocus and think of an appropriate response.

Stop Being Too Careful

People with social anxiety often think twice before saying something. Since they constantly worry about how others perceive them, they play it safe. Some people would rather stay quiet or avoid socialization than say something and have people judge or dislike them. Being careful every now and then can be beneficial and prevent you from saying the wrong thing. However, when you are always careful, you will feel more anxious and prevent others from getting to know you.

Let go and be more carefree. Although this can be very scary, it's quite liberating. Practice with people you are comfortable with first. Be yourself, let your guard down, and don't overthink everything you say. After gaining more confidence, try this tactic with strangers or co-workers. You will establish deep connections when you take social risks and be yourself around others. People can notice if you are pretending or aren't being your most authentic self.

Being more carefree will raise your self-confidence. When you see how people respond to you and enjoy your company, you will believe in yourself and your social skills. You will understand that you don't have to be perfect or always say the right thing for others to like you. No one expects you to be perfect. If you say something silly, laugh it off, and if you accidentally offend someone, apologize genuinely and make it clear you had no intention to offend them. Remember, you are still learning, so don't be hard on yourself.

Poor Social Skills

Approaching anyone and starting a conversation without messing up or saying the wrong thing is the dream. However, poor social skills can get in the way. No one is born social or suave, but you can work on yourself and develop these skills.

Practice

Can you learn to play the piano without practice? Developing social skills requires constantly working on yourself to improve and feel more confident. Push yourself and get out of your comfort zone. Start a conversation with the barista when you buy your coffee in the morning, your Uber driver, the bank teller, or the cashier at the supermarket. Ask them about their day or comment on the weather. Practice every chance you get with your co-workers, neighbors, or strangers on the bus. Even if you mess up or say something wrong, you can try the next day again. Making mistakes and learning from them is how you grow.

Make Eye Contact

Lack of eye contact is a clear sign you are nervous or uncomfortable. One of the most effective social skills you should master is making eye contact. According to a study by psychologist Thalia Wheatley, making eye contact sparks the attention of both individuals during a conversation. Imagine having a conversation with someone looking at their phone the whole time. You will feel they aren't being attentive. Making eye contact shows respect and that you are paying attention to what the other person is saying.

Learning to make eye contact allows people to become more comfortable with you.
https://unsplash.com/photos/M4MHtHVVS1E

Set a rule to make eye contact 70% of the time when the other person is talking and 50% when you are the one speaking. You might find eye contact uncomfortable if you are shy or struggle with self-confidence. Start small by making eye contact for a few seconds, then look away. Increase the duration each time until you feel at ease. If direct eye contact makes you uncomfortable, look at their eyebrows instead.

Visualize

Visualization is a powerful technique that makes people believe in themselves and improve their skills. Close your eyes now and imagine yourself in a social situation. What do you see? You probably see yourself sitting in a corner, avoiding people or messing up and embarrassing yourself. Again, this image isn't real. By visualizing yourself as a confident person with excellent social skills, you replace this image with a more powerful one. Take a few minutes daily, sit in a quiet room without distractions, and imagine yourself conversing with someone. You are funny, charming, and confident, and the other person smiles and engages in the conversation. Focus on every detail, like what you are wearing, tone of voice, body language, and what you are saying. In time, you can believe this image and act like it.

Find a Role Model

You can learn social skills by observing people in your life and emulating their behavior. Find a friend, co-worker, or family member with excellent social skills and notice how they approach people, start a conversation, and make small talk. Spend time with them to learn their techniques, and their behavior will rub off on you. If this is someone you are close to, ask them for advice on how to improve your social skills.

Set Goals

You can't improve your social skills if you remain in your comfort zone. Set goals to encourage yourself to socialize and practice small talk. At least once a month, attend a social event or gathering. Even if you still feel uncomfortable approaching people, stop and observe how they interact with each other; eventually, you'll get the courage to talk to someone.

Ensure you speak up once during every work meeting, whether to share an opinion or an idea. Stop ordering your meals online and make phone calls instead. Although these goals may seem small, they are a good start and can ease you in until you develop good social skills. Small goals are easier to achieve than big, unattainable ones that could set you up for failure.

Once you feel comfortable, set bigger goals. For instance, introduce yourself to two people at the next social event or do volunteer work and interact with others.

Low Self-Esteem

More often than not, a lack of self-esteem has held you back. How you see and think of yourself impacts all areas of your life. High self-esteem changes how you feel about yourself and the world around you. During conversations and interactions with others, focus on your positive qualities and remind yourself that you are just as interesting as anyone else.

Silence Your Inner Critic

Each person has an inner voice that either lifts them up and cheers for them or tears them down. If you have low self-esteem, you probably have an inner critic reminding you of your flaws and convincing you that you aren't good enough. It can prevent you from starting a conversation with others by focusing on what can go wrong or making you feel bad about yourself. Confident people have learned to handle this voice and not let it ruin their lives. Negative thoughts can destroy your self-esteem. However, you can challenge and weaken them by introducing positive and opposite thoughts to change your attitude.

Challenge these thoughts by questioning them. For instance, if your inner critic says you will make a fool of yourself when you talk to someone at a party, ask yourself, "When have I ever looked silly or embarrassed during a conversation?" You will realize that this has never happened or wasn't as bad as your thoughts make you believe.

Be aware of this voice and its impact on your self-esteem. Constantly challenge and question it until it goes away.

Don't Dwell on Your Mistakes

Everyone makes mistakes during social interactions. However, when you don't feel confident, your brain exaggerates your mistakes and makes you question yourself. Accept your imperfections and forgive yourself. If you say something stupid to your Uber driver, don't dwell on it. You will never see this person again, and they will most likely forget the interaction. Each time your brain brings up a past mistake, say "stop" out loud or under your breath. This is a very effective tactic that will shift your thoughts to the present moment instead of reliving something that already happened and with no impact on your present.

Take control of your thoughts instead of allowing them to control you. The next time your brain brings up a past mistake, quickly think of a fun social interaction where people praised you or enjoyed your company. Accept that you will always make mistakes. Don't let them define you or impact your self-worth.

Focus on Your Good Qualities

Low self-esteem prevents you from seeing your good qualities and how wonderful you are. In your diary or phone, write down everything you love about yourself, being sure to include compliments and lovely comments people have given you over the years. If you can't think of anything, ask your best friend, parents, or siblings for help. They will highlight your positive traits and what they love about spending time with you. Ask them to write them down so you can look at them every time your negative thoughts take over. Note your healthy and good habits or hobbies since they reflect your personality. For instance, if you eat healthily and exercise, you are smart and understand the significance of leading a healthy lifestyle. If you love reading, you are an intelligent person. Remember to read this list daily to constantly remind yourself of your exceptional qualities.

Introversion

Introverts hate small talk because they prefer deep conversations. Unlike social anxiety, poor social skills, and low self-esteem, introversion isn't an issue but a quality. You don't have to stop being an introvert. Merely learn to overcome your fear of small talk and understand its significance in daily interactions.

Be Approachable

People who don't understand introversion may assume that you are a snob or uninterested in engaging in a conversation. Introverts can initially be quiet, especially around people they don't know very well. Since they dislike small talk, introverts can seem bored during a conversation, making people think they don't want to talk. When interacting with people you don't know, offer a genuine smile and a warm attitude. It will make you seem approachable, putting people at ease around you. Even if you struggle with starting a conversation, walk into the room smiling; that's an invitation for people to come to talk to you!

Reward Yourself

Treat yourself to something you like every time you make small talk with someone. For instance, tell yourself that if you make small talk with two people today, you will buy yourself a nice dinner or spend the evening reading the book you just bought. The reward should be something you enjoy doing. However, if you fail, punish yourself. For instance, don't binge-watch the new season of your favorite show, or don't play video games for a week. Creating a reward and punishment system will motivate you to get out of your comfort zone and approach people.

Your thoughts hold you back. Whether you are an introvert or have social anxiety, low self-esteem, or poor social skills, your negative thoughts have tricked you into believing you can't make small talk or that people will find you boring. Understanding that these thoughts aren't honest (and only playing on your insecurities) is crucial; they are like the scary stories of Bigfoot you heard as a child. They are unreal and defy logic. Replacing them with positive and healthy thoughts is your first and most significant step to overcoming these struggles, so you can eventually talk to anyone effortlessly and confidently.

Be yourself. You have much to offer, *even if you don't believe it.* Don't let your inner critic win. Keep reminding yourself of your good qualities and how people enjoy your company. Believe that this inner voice will not have power over you without your permission. Approach people with a smile and a friendly attitude. Even if you feel nervous, smiling will relax you and make others comfortable, giving you the courage to engage with them. Remember, you are who you believe you are, so *believe* you are a confident and interesting person.

Chapter 3: Small Talk Tricks for the Introvert

Small talk is often one of the more tiresome aspects of networking events. It's an essential part of meeting people and making new acquaintances. While extroverts thrive on sharing their stories and getting to know people, introverts often find small talk stressful. It can be challenging for introverts to jump into conversations and start building rapport. Instead, they prefer to listen and observe before they engage with others.

Small talk is a key factor for successful networking.
https://unsplash.com/photos/ZDN-G1xBWHY

Introverts are not necessarily shy and can be quite outgoing *in their own way*. The difference is that they need to feel comfortable before they open up and share themselves with others. Therefore, small talk can be more of a challenge for introverts than for extroverts. The good news is there are ways to make small talk easier for introverts. By understanding what makes them tick and how they can work with their unique personality traits, introverts can learn to navigate social situations and build rapport with others. If you're an introvert, here are eight techniques to help you work with your personality and become a better small talker.

Reduce Anxiety

Anxiety can make even the simplest conversations feel like a challenge. In 2008, researchers attempted to determine whether people with Social Anxiety Disorder (SAD) are less skilled in social interactions or if it is all in their heads. In an article published in the Journal of Anxiety Disorders, the authors concluded that the difference in performance might be due to anxiety and not only skill level. In other words, if you have anxiety about small talk, it can make it seem like an insurmountable challenge. A few techniques can help reduce your stress and make small talk easier:

Start Small

If you're new to the world of small talk, don't jump right into a conversation with a stranger at a party. Start with the people you know well – perhaps coworkers or classmates – and ask them how their day was. If they're chatty, ask more questions about their lives. If not, ask what they think about an upcoming event or news story in the headlines.

When you feel ready to branch out, start with someone who seems friendly and approachable. Don't force yourself to find common ground if you don't have anything to say, but keep the conversation going by asking questions. Asking open-ended questions is an easy way to get people to talk. Instead of asking, "How are you?" ask, "What's new with your job?" or even, "Tell me about yourself." If you're at a loss for words, comment on something in their environment; their clothes or accessories are easy conversation starters.

Ace Introductions

The first step toward making excellent small talk is to know how to introduce yourself. The best way is with a statement that gives your name and why you're talking to them. For example, "Hi, my name is Bob, and I was wondering if you could help me with something?" This introduction invites people into the conversation because they know what you want from them.

When you make an introduction, asking if the person is free to talk is always a good idea. For example, "Do you have a minute? I want to ask you something." This question shows you respect their time and allows them to decline your request if they don't have time for this conversation.

If they have time, ask them if discussing a particular topic is okay. For example, "Do you mind if we talk about your salary for a minute?" Notice how this question prepares the person for what's coming next and doesn't come across as pushy or demanding.

Use Self-Help Tools

Self-help tools are designed to help you manage your anxiety and stress and can be a great way to help you feel more comfortable when you're nervous. A self-help tool can be a physical object, like a stress ball, journal, or a simple mantra you say to yourself when stressed. You can say these phrases to yourself when you are anxious:

- "My anxiety is just a feeling, and it won't hurt me."
- "I can do this."
- "It's okay if I make mistakes."
- "It's okay if I don't know what to say or do. I can just listen."
- "It's important to start a conversation with someone at networking events. That person probably won't know many people there and will appreciate another person to talk with."

Notice Body Language

Nonverbal cues, like facial expressions and gestures, can affect how a person interprets what you say during small talk. It may come across as unfriendly or defensive if you're standing or sitting with your arms crossed over your chest. Instead, open up and lean forward slightly when talking with someone; this will make you seem more open and interested in what they are saying.

Small Talk Is More than Trivial Topics

The outcome of your small talk depends largely on your attitude. Don't view it as a waste of time. Instead, think of small talk as an opportunity to connect with someone and show interest in them. Small talk can create an opening for more meaningful conversations later. Before chatting with someone you don't know, ask yourself, "How can I make our conversation interesting?" Objectives help introverts channel their focus in concrete ways. Knowing your goals makes it easier to determine how you'll achieve them.

Ask yourself what you want to get out of the conversation. Do you want to make a good impression on someone? Find out more about them and their interests. Start a new friendship with someone with similar values. Even if you need to figure out your objectives, having a few is a good idea. You can always revise them as the conversation progresses.

Your objective doesn't have to be a specific outcome. For example, you can make a good impression on someone by showing you care about what they are saying and are interested in getting to know them better. If so, think of how you can demonstrate this. Ask them about their hobbies or find out what they like and dislike about their job. You can also make a good impression by being upbeat and friendly. If you're trying to start a new friendship, share some common interests with the other person. If you're looking for a new job, get advice from the person you're talking with and show that you are willing to work hard and learn new skills.

Channel Your Curiosity

Curiosity can turn small talk into a gratifying experience where two people learn more about one another. While introverts seem quiet or shy, they are merely different from extroverts in how their brains absorb information. You'll likely not ask a hundred questions at a dinner party if you're an introvert. Still, if you're curious about something, you will ask a few questions.

Use your curiosity to engage in small talk. Ask questions that aren't too personal or invasive. Instead, get insight into what the other person enjoys doing and why they enjoy it. Ask questions that come to mind while listening attentively to their answers.

Lead the Conversation

Making contact by saying "Hello" is easy, but keeping a conversation going takes skill. Introverts usually withdraw when they feel uncomfortable in a social situation. However, to lead a discussion, you must be in it, no matter how small. The key to making a conversation flow is to know when to lead and when to listen. The following tips will help you lead the flow of small talk:

Be Yourself

When introverts try to lead conversations, they often sound like they're trying too hard, which isn't natural or authentic. The key is not to try so hard that you sound fake or unnatural. Instead, just be yourself. This way, people will recognize when you're opening up and being authentic.

If you're unsure how to do this, think about what makes you unique. You might have a funny story about something that happened at work or school or a movie quote that always comes up when someone asks you what's new. These things set you apart from everyone else and are perfect for small talk.

Ask Directed Questions

Leading a conversation is about asking questions, but not any random question will do. A good question must be directed and specific, like, "What's your favorite place to go for coffee?" or "Have you been here before?" These questions allow the other person to share information about themselves while also helping them feel comfortable talking with you.

Ask Questions That Demonstrate Interest

If someone says they're taking Spanish classes, ask them how they like it. They'll feel more connected with you and share more information if they know they've got someone who cares about what they're learning.

If someone tells you they've just moved to town, ask what brought them there. Ask about their outfit or jewelry if you want to start a conversation with a stranger at an event or party. It gives both of you an easy topic to discuss and helps break the ice.

Make Statements about What Is Around You

Making statements about what's around often helps open up the conversation. Make comments relevant to the situation and likely to interest the other person, such as "Wow, this ice cream is delicious." or "It feels so good out here tonight." You could ask what they think about certain things (like your outfit or jewelry), which should get them talking again.

Make Statements about Yourself

One of the best ways to get a conversation going again when someone has stopped talking is to make statements about yourself. A statement can be as simple as saying, "Oh, you like that band too?" or "I was thinking about getting those sunglasses." These comments are usually safe because they're not too personal and don't require much commitment from the other person.

If someone asks you a question, answer it briefly and bring the conversation back to them. For example, if someone asks how old you are, answer briefly and then say, "But what about you? What's your story?"

Provide an Outlet for Them to Talk

If you're not asking questions, at least provide an outlet for the other person to talk. It could be as simple as nodding your head and saying "mm-hmm" or "yeah" when they say something interesting or informative. You don't have to say anything, but knowing they have someone listening will make it easier for them to open up.

Make Your Responses Interesting and Engaging

Small talk can abruptly stop if you give uninteresting responses to the person's questions. If they ask how your weekend was, don't say "fine" and leave it at that. Give a few details. Say, "It was great because my friends and I went hiking in the mountains. We climbed to the top of the tallest peak and saw awesome views." That's a much better response than "It was fine."

You can also ask questions back, making the conversation flow more smoothly. If they start talking about their weekend, ask them what they did and how it went. This way, you don't have to come up with something else to say. They're giving you the information you can respond to.

It's important to remember that not every conversation has to go smoothly. Sometimes, you have awkward silence, or the other person will say something odd or off-topic. In these cases, don't panic. The best thing to do is acknowledge it and move on. For example, suppose they say something unrelated to the topic of discussion. In that case, you could say, "Yeah....," (with a puzzled expression) and continue talking about whatever came before. Alternatively, if they ask you a question and you don't know how to answer, *say so*; don't fake it or make up an answer. The easiest way to handle this situation is to say, "I don't know," or "I don't have an opinion on that yet." It may feel like you're being honest but not helpful, but it will give them a chance to come up with a solution instead of relying on yours.

Deepen the Conversation

The quality of your questions helps you keep the conversation going. Instead of asking "yes or no" questions, ask "why?" or "how?" questions. These questions are more open-ended and will give your partner a chance to explain their reasoning instead of giving you a simple answer. For example, if someone asks you, "What's your favorite movie?" and you say, "Star Wars," the conversation could end there. However, if they ask, "Why do you like Star Wars so much?" or "How did it make you feel when Luke Skywalker was training with Yoda on Dagobah for the first time?" this opens up new avenues of discussion that might not have been available otherwise.

The crux of small talk is to distill what someone is saying to its core to understand what is important to them. It helps you learn more about each other and avoids awkward moments where one person feels they have nothing else to talk about. If you are in a group setting, be the person who starts conversations. If there is an awkward silence, don't let it stand; take matters into your hands and say something. You will get out of your shell and make people feel more comfortable around you because they know that if they don't have anything to contribute, you do.

Recognize Non-Verbal Cues

To be a good conversationalist, you must learn to read people's non-verbal cues. Body language (the movements and positions of the body) can tell how someone feels about what they are saying or how they feel about what is happening around them. With practice, you can learn to respond when given social cues appropriately. When engaging in small talk with someone, look out for the following non-verbal cues:

Facial Expressions

If the person is smiling and laughing, they are probably having a good time. If they frown or look serious, change the subject or conversation tone.

If you notice someone's eyebrows are raised, they might be surprised or confused by what was said. It could be an opportunity to clarify what was meant by your statement or ask questions about why they seem so surprised.

Kinesics

Kinesic communication studies non-verbal behavior, like gestures and facial expressions. If you're an introvert, you might struggle in social situations that call for small talk. However, there are ways to lead the conversation without having to speak.

For example, looking at your watch or your phone every few minutes gives the impression you're not engaged in what other people are saying. However, if you look up and make eye contact with the person talking to you, they'll assume you're listening and interested in what they are saying. It's also a good idea to pay attention to body language. If someone crosses their arms or taps their foot when they get nervous or uncomfortable, it gives them a chance to catch their breath before starting the next sentence.

Another way to look at it is to nod your head and say "Mmm-hmm" or "Yes, go on" when someone is talking. It shows you're listening and interested in what they are saying and encourages them to keep going.

Be a Student of Great Conversationalists

Great conversationalists are like great artists; they've developed a keen eye for detail and an ability to see things differently than most people. You must study those great conversational artists to become a better conversationalist yourself!. Listen closely as your friends talk about their lives or what they read in the news, pay attention when you meet new people who seem particularly interesting or charismatic, and take note of how your favorite TV shows or movies are written.

You'll notice that great conversations are about more than words; they're also about energy and body language. They have a natural flow that keeps people engaged and wanting more. Moreover, they take place in the present moment. You'll never hear a great conversationalist say, "Back in my day..." or "Remember when you could buy a house for $50,000?" Instead, they focus on what is happening right now. This is not to say that you shouldn't discuss the past or the future. It helps you avoid giving a generic response, which is what most people do when asked about something from the past. They offer a one-line answer like, "I thought it was great" or "It wasn't that good." That doesn't engage people or make them want to continue with small talk.

Expand on your answer when you are asked a question about the past. Explain why you thought it was great or not so good. It can be as simple as: "Yes, I thought it was great because we had fun together and made new friends." This response engages people in conversation because they want to know more about what happened.

Create a Reward System

As an introvert, sometimes all it takes is a little push to get you to take the plunge and start talking. A simple way is to create a reward system. For example, if you speak to five people at the party, you'll get a free dessert, or every time someone asks you a question and you answer, they owe you one dollar (in your mind, of course!) The key is that the reward must be small and tangible. You can't say, "I'll feel better about myself" as your reward because this won't motivate you to do anything specific.

If you need a little help coming up with ideas for your reward system, ask yourself some questions: What do I like to do? What would make me feel good right now? Is there anything specific I want to accomplish at this party that requires talking to people? Once you have an idea of your reward, write it down and place it somewhere visible so you'll remember.

Finally, write down a few things that you want to avoid. These are the behaviors detrimental to your social success at this party. Examples include:

- Hiding in the corner and avoiding eye contact with everyone
- Ignoring people who attempt to talk to you
- Acting like an introvert (leaving early, not speaking up when with conversations around you)

As an introvert, you may be harsh on yourself if a particular encounter does not turn out as you hoped. If you had a bad encounter at the party, don't dwell on it or beat yourself up. Instead, think about what could have been done differently to make things go smoother. Practice these tips before future social gatherings so they become second nature. Also, remember, you are not alone in feeling this way. Many introverts feel the same way about socializing as you do. It is difficult to overcome your shyness, but seeing how much pleasure and benefit there is in making small talk is worth learning how to do it.

Chapter 4: Do: The Best Small Talk Topics

Small talk can be one of the most intimidating aspects of any social interaction. After all, what do you say if you don't know anyone there? It can quickly become awkward and uncomfortable without suitable topics to discuss. This is why getting familiar with some of the best small talk topics is essential to keep conversations flowing and ensure everyone has a good time. This chapter covers some of the best topics for small talk and how you can use them in everyday conversations.

It helps to make notes of small talk topics that you can bring up in conversation.
https://unsplash.com/photos/xxHDLWmc1wE

How to Choose the Best Small Talk Topics

Small talk topics can range from lighthearted and casual to more serious. Choosing the right topic for any conversation depends on various factors, including who you're talking to, the context of the conversation, and your comfort level with different topics.

Read the Room

One way to determine which small talk topics best suit a particular situation is to observe what other people are discussing. Bringing up sports is a good idea if it is a topic of discussion among everyone. It ensures your conversations will fit in. Knowing the social context of a situation is vital to choosing suitable topics.

Know Your Audience

If you're in a more formal or professional setting, stick to less controversial topics, such as current events, local attractions, and hobbies. On the other hand, if you're talking with friends or family members, feel free to talk about anything that interests you. Regardless of who you're talking to, picking topics to create an open and friendly atmosphere is vital.

Lighthearted Topics

Many people enjoy discussing lighthearted topics during small talk conversations. These topics could include books or movies they recently read or watched, upcoming plans for the weekend, recent vacation destinations, or funny stories. Lighthearted topics are a great way to break the ice and keep the conversation going.

The Comfort Zone

Another essential factor to consider for small talk topics is how comfortable you feel discussing certain subjects. If a topic makes you uncomfortable, it's best to avoid bringing it up and instead opt for one more familiar. You will ensure the conversation runs smoothly without awkward pauses or moments of tension.

Play to Your Strengths

If you're more comfortable talking about books than movies, ensure it is the topic you bring up in conversations. When you are confident with the subject, everyone involved feels at ease and can naturally move on to other topics if necessary. It makes the conversation more interesting for both parties as they learn something new or explore a different angle on a familiar topic.

Relate to Each Other

It's always essential to find common ground with your conversational partner. If they mention a shared experience or interest, then use that as an opportunity to dive deeper into the conversation and connect. Ask questions about their experiences and find deeper shared values. Striking up a conversation about something that interests you both is the best way to build trust and rapport. By showing genuine interest in the other person, they'll be more likely to open up and have an enjoyable conversation.

Finally, remember to be yourself. People can tell when you're not genuine, so your conversations must be natural and authentic. Don't be afraid to show your true colors; after all, engaging conversations are all about making meaningful connections with other people.

The Most Common Small Talk Topics

The art of small talk is one of the most vital skills you can learn, especially if you want to make a great impression. Whether it's networking events, first dates, or conversations with strangers, small talk can help break the ice and lead to meaningful conversations.

No matter the situation, small talk topics are essential for meaningful conversation. Choosing the right one creates an environment where everyone feels included, and conversations naturally flow. Knowing which topics to bring up in different settings and playing to your strengths can go a long way toward creating enjoyable conversations with friends, family, or even strangers.

Now that you know the basics, let's look at some of the best small talk topics you can bring up in any situation.

Movies and TV Shows

Movies and TV shows are great subjects to start a conversation. With so many genres, streaming services, and endless content available, everyone has something in common they can talk about - be it the latest blockbuster or an old favorite.

Binge-watching has become increasingly popular over the past few years, with streaming services like Netflix offering entire seasons of shows at once. So it is easy to watch multiple episodes in one sitting. As a result, many people will enjoy discussing their favorite shows and debating those worth watching. When binge-watching is a small talk topic, you could ask questions like, "What have been your favorite series to binge-watch?" or "What do you think is the best series currently on Netflix?" Do you prefer comedies or dramas?

Everyone loves a great movie, and new films are constantly being released – and this is something people enjoy discussing. The great question is, "What are the best films to watch?" You could take it a step further by asking what the other person's favorite movies of all time are or what recent releases have been their favorite. These questions can lead you down an interesting path and provide plenty of topics for conversation.

Discussing trailers in more detail can fuel conversation. You can talk about your first impressions, speculate on plot points or get excited about what looks likely to be a great movie. Talking about trailers is a great way to stay in the loop on what's coming out and provides plenty of conversation starters for those who love movies. It's always a great way to get people talking and often leads to other topics of conversation.

Social Media

Social media has become an integral part of our lives, so it's no wonder it's a popular topic for small talk. You can start conversations about the latest trends or features or ask which platform they prefer and why. Discussing how people use social media can be a great way to get to know someone better. Asking about their favorite accounts or influencers is an excellent entry point into more meaningful conversations.

Music

If you're a music aficionado, discussing your favorite genre or band can be the perfect way to start a conversation. Talking about music tastes gives you much insight into someone's personality and interests. From indie rock to rap, there's undoubtedly something both parties can enjoy discussing. Ask questions about what songs they like, their favorite artists, and why they love them so much. Share stories from concerts you've attended or albums with special memories attached to them.

Live performances are another great way to talk about music with others. Going to concerts provides opportunities to bond over shared experiences, and discussing past shows is a fun way to reminisce on memories. Ask each other about recent concerts. "Have you been to any great shows lately?" or "What's the best show you've ever seen?"

Lastly, music videos are a great topic to explore. Music videos provide insight into the artist's creative vision and style. Talk about the video's visuals in color, lighting, and other elements. Does the video have an overall message or theme? What do you think they were trying to convey with their artistry? You could watch it together for fun and see if anything unusual or amusing jumps out at you. If it's a humorous video, take the opportunity to laugh together at the jokes and make silly comments about what's happening in the scene. Whether your music tastes lean towards classic rock or EDM, discussing music can be a great way to get to know someone better.

Sports and Fitness

Sports and fitness are great conversation topics to get to know someone at any level. Whether it's talking about our favorite teams, players, or sports moments, discussing exercise routines, tips for getting in shape, or recapping past events and upcoming competitions, these conversations can open up an entire world of possibilities.

Regarding teams and players, there is so much to talk about. What teams do you like? Who are your favorite players? How long have you been following them? What was the most exciting game or moment with them? These questions could lead to some fascinating conversations lasting hours!

Workouts and exercise are another great way to start a conversation. You can talk about what exercise you do or even ask the person to give you some tips on staying in shape. Compare your exercise routines and discuss techniques to help each other.

Talking about upcoming competitions and events or recapping past ones is an excellent chance to get people to chat. It's fun to speculate on who will win and why or relive the exciting moments from previous games. These conversations are not only entertaining but can also be very educational.

Travel

Another fun topic of conversation is travel. People love talking about their favorite places they've visited or want to visit. You can ask questions about what places they like to explore, where they've been, and which places have left an impression on them. If you have not traveled much, it's a great way to learn more about different cultures, cities, and lifestyles worldwide. You can discuss upcoming trips or what activities people like to do while traveling. Do they prefer sightseeing or lounging on the beach? What foods do they enjoy in different countries?

You could talk about what type of traveler they are or share tips on seeing a particular destination. If you have similar tastes in travel experiences, use this opportunity to discuss trips you could take together.

Talking about food is another fun topic related to travel. Ask questions like: What cuisines did you try? Did you get any recommendations from locals on where to eat? Did you come across any interesting dishes that surprised you? These questions allow both parties to share their experiences and exchange food stories. Whether you're discussing future travel plans, past trips, or just hearing about the different places someone has been to, talking about traveling is always an interesting conversation starter.

The Weather

One of the most common conversation topics is talking about the weather – a lighter topic that could prompt interesting conversations. Start by asking what climate they prefer and why; it could lead to an in-depth discussion about their favorite places, activities, or climates.

Talk about what season they like best, winter or summer. "How do you like to spend your time when it is cold outside?" or "How do you usually spend your summers?" It could be an excellent opportunity to plan outdoor activities together.

If you're feeling adventurous, bring up wild weather topics, like tornadoes or hurricanes. Ask them questions like: "Have you ever been in a tornado?" or "What's the craziest storm you've ever seen?" These topics will spark a lot of exciting stories.

Family

Family is an incredibly essential topic and can be a great conversation starter. You could start by asking how many siblings they have, what their parents do for work, or even reminiscing about the funniest moments with family members. It's an excellent opportunity to discuss family traditions or stories passed down through generations. "How do you remember your childhood?" or "Do you have any favorite family recipes?"

You could chat about past family vacations and the craziest things during those trips and ask them to share funny stories from those experiences. Talk about each family member's traditions; this will let you know more of their personal history and build a closer bond with them.

Discussing upcoming holidays or other special occasions like birthdays and anniversaries can bring people together in the conversation. Ask them questions like: "What's your favorite holiday?" or "How do you usually celebrate special occasions with your family?" Family can be a good opportunity to break the ice. Ask them about the most amusing things their parents did when they were kids, or compare and contrast different parenting styles. Who knows? You might even get a few new ideas for your own family.

Work

Work can be a great conversation starter, especially when discussing professional endeavors. Ask them questions like, "What project are you currently working on?" or "What do you see yourself doing in the future in your career?" Work will help get the conversation going and allow you to learn more about each other's ambitions and goals.

It will give you a chance to offer advice or support that could help them reach their goals. Another great topic of work is work and private life balance. This is a crucial issue for most people, so talking about navigating your workload while still finding time for yourself and your loved ones can be a real bonding experience. Who knows, maybe there's something you can learn from each other to make the most out of life.

Celebrity Gossip

Celebrity gossip is always a fun topic to discuss. It's exciting to keep up with the latest releases and trends that celebrities are participating in. When discussing new releases, you could start by discussing what movies have recently come out or what songs are topping the charts. Ask questions like: "What did you think about the latest movie release?" or "Do you have a favorite song from this album?" Getting to know each other's tastes is great.

Talking about awards shows is another fun conversation starter. Ask: Who do you think should have won an award at the show? What were some of the most memorable moments? What did you think of the performances?

Talk about fashion trends that celebrities are rocking. Discuss what's trending in terms of streetwear or on the red carpet. Ask questions, "Who do you think had the best outfit at the show?" and "What was your favorite look from this season's collection?"

Technology

Technology is a great topic to discuss with someone, as it's constantly evolving and can open up many interesting conversations. You can talk about the latest gadgets, software advancements, or even your favorite apps.

When discussing gadgets, ask what hardware they own. What's their experience been like with this device? What do they think are its strengths and weaknesses? You could enjoy lively debates about which devices are the best or why certain features should be considered when shopping for a new one.

Regarding software and applications, talking about current trends or recent updates can get people to share their opinions on specific programs or services. There could be an app you both use regularly or one that recently caught your eye. Compare the features of each and discuss which one's better for specific tasks.

Social Media Platforms are another great topic to explore when discussing technology. What platforms do you use? How active are you on them? Have these apps changed how people interact with each other or influenced their daily lives? It is interesting to hear people's different perspectives and learn new ways of using existing tools.

Hobbies

Hobbies are excellent conversation starters and for getting to know someone deeper. Ask them what they enjoy doing in their free time, such as reading, writing, playing sports, or hiking. You can even ask specific questions about the activities that interest them most. For example, "What sort of literature gets your pages turning?" and "What sport do you play?"

Discuss pastimes you share in common. When you talk about you can instantly bond over shared interests and experiences. Inquire of them, "What's the best part of your (hobby)?" or "How long have you been doing this?" Follow up with discussion points about your hobbies so that you can share stories and experiences.

Hometown

Discussing hometowns always becomes interesting when you learn more about someone's roots and culture. Ask them questions like: "What do you miss most about your hometown?" or "What are some of the landmarks people should visit if they ever go there?" You will understand their origins and what makes them unique.

Discuss changes in their hometown over the years, how it has evolved, and how it has changed their lives. Talking about past experiences and memories can be a great bonding experience for both parties. It gives you ideas on places to visit when traveling. Local Cuisine is a great topic to bring up when talking about hometowns - what are their favorite dishes and restaurants? You can always ask if they have any hidden gems you should check out.

Everyone has a unique story, and it's your job to listen and engage. The more you know about someone's hometown, the more you can connect with them emotionally. So, don't be afraid to ask questions - get curious and explore.

Health

Health is an important topic to discuss when talking with others. You can talk about nutrition and diet, mental well-being, or exercise routines. Discuss what foods are best for your body, how to stay healthy and maintain your mental well-being, and explore different exercise routines to help people to keep fit and healthy.

Ask questions like, "What fitness routine do you follow?" or "Do you have any advice for a healthier lifestyle?" These questions help you gain insight into someone's health habits and could give you some helpful tips on staying healthy. Discuss the importance of mental health and how to maintain it. For instance, ask, "What helps you stay positive?" or "What do you do when feeling overwhelmed?" This encourages positive dialogue about mental health and creates a safe space for both parties to express their thoughts.

The conversation is about connection. Regardless of what topics you choose to discuss with someone, it's necessary to be open-minded and respectful. The goal is to get to know each other better, so keep an open mind and listen actively – try not to focus too much on any one topic.

Lastly, remember conversation should always be a two-way street. After you've asked questions about their hobbies, hometowns, or health, you must also offer your stories. This creates a balanced dialogue that encourages meaningful exchange and connection between both parties.

Chapter 5: Don't: The Worst Small Talk Topics

Everyone knows how to make small talk and have some go-to topics to discuss to break the ice and start a conversation. It's one of those social rules ingrained in them since childhood. But what happens when the conversation gets a little too personal? Many topics are inappropriate for light conversation with a stranger. If you are veering into one of these uncomfortable areas, the best course of action is to steer the conversation in a different direction.

Knowing what not to talk about is crucial to conversation.
https://www.pexels.com/photo/woman-wearing-teal-dress-sitting-on-chair-talking-to-man-2422280/

What Not to Talk About

Knowing what is considered appropriate conversation material when talking to someone you don't know can be challenging. It's best to avoid discussing topics that may be too personal, controversial, or sensitive to avoid awkward or uncomfortable conversations. This chapter explores the worst small talk topics and how to avoid them.

Politics

One of the most notorious small-talk topics to avoid is politics. It can be challenging to bring up political topics politely and respectfully, especially when talking to someone who might not share your views. Political conversations can quickly become heated and are best kept out of the realm of small talk. Instead, focus on topics that bring people together, such as shared hobbies, music preferences, or travel experiences. Doing so helps create a more positive atmosphere and provides better opportunities to get to know someone. No matter the topic of conversation, it's essential to be mindful and courteous when talking with a stranger. Listening carefully and asking thoughtful questions shows you are genuinely interested in the other person. A respectful dialogue will help prevent political topics from turning into an argument and allow you to connect on a more meaningful level.

Religion

Religion is another conversation topic that can quickly become uncomfortable. Different cultures and religions usually have different beliefs, so discussing their differences in detail is inappropriate for small talk. For example, when discussing religion with a stranger, it's best to focus on the commonalities between different beliefs rather than debating over differences. It's also important to avoid discussing controversial topics related to religion, like politics or morality. Even if you have strong opinions on these issues, sharing them during small talk is inappropriate. Instead, focus on expressing support for the person's beliefs and asking questions in a non-judgmental way. You will create a respectful and pleasant atmosphere for the conversation.

While it's best to avoid discussing religion during small talk, it can be difficult sometimes. If you notice the conversation turning to religious topics, being sensitive and mindful of the other person's beliefs is important. Respectfully acknowledge their faith, but take steps to steer the conversation back toward more appropriate topics. This way, both parties can enjoy a pleasant and respectful dialogue without feeling uncomfortable or judged.

Money and Debt

Money is a topic that should be avoided in small talk. Discussing personal finances can make even the most confident person feel anxious or embarrassed. Additionally, it can be in poor taste and make the other person uncomfortable. It is best to avoid money-related topics altogether when engaging in small talk. If the other person brings it up, focus on broad topics like economic trends or current events rather than delving into personal matters. You can talk about inflation and job markets without getting too personal. This way, you stay away from the more sensitive aspects of money and still have an enjoyable, engaging conversation.

Likewise, it is impolite to ask the other person what they do for a living unless it is clear they are okay with talking about their job. Avoid topics like salary or how much things cost. It is also best to avoid discussing investments and tax plans, as these can be very sensitive topics. Instead, focus on the positive aspects of work and deter from anything too personal.

You may be tempted to talk about stocks or other investments that have worked for you. However, this can make the other person feel inadequate or excluded. The key is to focus on broad topics that are not too personal or intrusive.

Remember, money should not be used as a barometer for someone's worth. Avoid making assumptions or judgments about someone's financial status. People of all income levels can be interesting and engaging conversation partners, so focus on finding common ground in other topics. Avoiding money-related discussions ensures everyone feels comfortable and included in the conversation.

Sex

Another topic to avoid in small talk is sex. It's a sensitive subject that is best discussed when both parties know each other considerably well. Even then, it should be done with caution and respect. The last thing you want to do is make someone feel uncomfortable, embarrassed, or judged.

It is not appropriate to make sexual advances or jokes during small talk. Remember, some cultures and religions have more conservative views on sex, so it's essential to be aware of the context and avoid mentioning it.

When talking with a stranger, it's best to keep conversations light and avoid discussing anything related to sex, including sexual orientation, sexual preferences, sexual experiences, relationships, and anything else that could be interpreted as offensive or inappropriate. If they raise the topic in conversation first, take your cues on how far you can go into this subject before finding an alternative topic of discussion.

Good manners and common sense will guide your conversations in these situations. By being mindful of your words and listening carefully, you can ensure your conversations remain light, friendly, and enjoyable.

Relationship Issues

Regarding small talk, relationship issues are most definitely off the table. Sharing details about your relationship or someone else's is a surefire way to create an awkward conversation. Relationship issues include discussing break-ups, family issues, or other sensitive topics that could make the person uncomfortable. Never bad mouth or complain about your partner, as this can be seen as disrespectful, especially if you have just met the person. Discussing your or someone else's relationship issues in small talk is inappropriate.

It's best to avoid these subjects altogether; instead, focus on more lighthearted topics. It's always polite to ask open-ended questions that invite the person to share positive stories or experiences rather than digging into potential triggering topics. Remember, offering a smile and showing kindness when talking to someone is always *welcoming*.

Dirty Jokes

Although dirty jokes are funny or entertaining to some, remember: *not everyone will find them appropriate.* It's best to steer clear of jokes that could be offensive or rude when engaging in small talk. It doesn't mean humor isn't welcome in small talk, but preferably it should be done respectfully and tastefully. Dirty jokes can make everyone laugh, but it's better to save them for friends and family where you know they will be appreciated.

Save the dirty jokes for more appropriate settings for a more successful and comfortable conversation. Not everyone has the same sense of humor, so be mindful of what jokes you tell. Small talk should be about finding common ground, so stick to topics that you and the other person can relate to positively.

Inside Jokes

Inside jokes are great for making friends and family laugh, but they shouldn't be used in conversations with strangers. Not only do people not understand them, but they can also feel left out or excluded. Inside jokes are not suited for small talk. They are jokes that only make sense to those who experienced the situation firsthand and can be off-putting to those not included. For instance, if you talk about a funny incident that happened to you and your friends, the other person won't get the joke and will have no idea what you're talking about. It could make them feel awkward or even offended.

The same goes for references to movies, TV shows, and other popular cultures. Not everyone will have seen the same movies as you or watched the same TV shows, so these references are usually lost on strangers. Similarly, slang and cultural references can be challenging to decipher for people from different backgrounds or parts of the world. Focus on topics everyone can relate to, like pop culture, current events, and sports.

Physical Appearances

It's generally best to avoid topics related to physical appearances during small talk. Avoid passing comments about someone's clothing, hair, makeup, or figure. These topics could be considered rude and intrusive, and it's possible you could deeply hurt the other person's feelings.

Complimenting someone on their physical appearance is one of the quickest ways to put them on the spot; even if it's a kind comment, it can still make them uncomfortable. Instead, focus on aspects of their personality or interests to show appreciation and make them feel good.

It's equally important to be aware of how your appearance could be interpreted. For example, if you're dressed particularly well or wearing a lot of makeup, it could be considered superiority or over-indulgence. If you're dressed too casually for the situation, it could be seen as disrespectful. Therefore, always dress and groom yourself so that you put everyone at ease.

By showing respect to others and knowing how your appearance could be interpreted, you can easily steer the conversation in a more appropriate direction. Ultimately, it's about creating a comfortable, welcoming, and mutual environment for all parties.

Past Relationships

When conversing with someone, avoiding talking about ex-partners or past relationships is best. Talking about divorce, break-ups, and complicated past relationships usually becomes an uncomfortable conversation and is likely to make the other person uneasy, especially if you don't know the person well.

Discussing domestic abuse or other emotional trauma that you or the other person has experienced is inappropriate and painful memories can quickly and unwantedly resurface. Instead, focus on getting to know the other person and refrain from chats that might make them uncomfortable. Respect their privacy and be mindful of the things you talk about. Should the topic arise, remember to be sensitive and kind. Keeping conversations light and enjoyable is the best way to make small talk a positive experience for both parties.

Some subjects are better left for deeper and more meaningful conversations with close friends or family. Remember, small talk should be light and friendly, so it is best to avoid heavy topics that could lead to an unpleasant conversation. Refraining from this topic will help ensure your interactions are enjoyable for everyone involved.

Kids

Children are a great source of joy in many people's lives, but talking about them in small talk conversations is not always the best idea. It feels awkward to ask someone how many kids they have or if they plan to have any. You don't know the person's family situation, so avoiding potentially sensitive topics is best.

Instead, focus on topics that relate to children without being too direct. A great way to talk about kids without getting too personal is to ask the person about parenting strategies like discipline or nutrition. You can ask about the person's favorite childhood memories. This opens up a conversation that could be an interesting and fun way to get to know someone better.

Similarly, talking about your children can make the other person feel excluded or not part of the conversation. Instead, talk about topics involving children more broadly. For instance, discussing current events involving kids or the latest educational trends.

Health Issues

Talking about death, illness, or any traumatic loss should not be taken lightly. It can be challenging to discuss as it often brings up difficult and painful emotions. Even if you know the person reasonably well, it is still inappropriate to bring up these topics. While it is possible to chat about death or grief sensitively, these conversations should generally be reserved for those particularly close to you. If you are talking to a stranger, it is best to avoid this discussion altogether.

Remember, many people struggle with mental health issues, and discussing it with someone you don't know very well can be triggering. If the topic of mental health or illness comes up, it's best to tread lightly and be sensitive to the other person's feelings.

This can be tricky when discussing health in general, as most people don't want to divulge too much about their medical issues. It's best to ask the person if they are comfortable discussing the topic before delving into it further. Everyone's health is a very confidential matter, and conversations about it can make the other person feel awkward or exposed, especially if they are dealing with more serious health issues.

Controversial Social Issues

Many controversial topics, like abortion or gun control, can be challenging. These conversations can become heated very quickly, so it is best to avoid them altogether when making small talk. Understanding that everyone has their own beliefs and opinions is important, so discussing them might not always lead to a pleasant conversation. Even if the other person agrees with you, they could feel attacked or uncomfortable if the discussion turns aggressive.

Many prefer not to give their point of view about LGBTQ+ rights, abortion, religion, voting issues, and racial topics in public or among strangers. They fear judgment and criticism or are not comfortable enough to engage in these discussions.

It's also worth noting that some people are more open about discussing sensitive topics than others. So, if the person is willing to engage in a respectful debate about one of these subjects, you can continue the conversation; however, it's best to switch the topic if you sense any tension. It is recommended not to broach controversial social issues during small talk to avoid potential discomfort or awkwardness.

Gossiping and Rumors

Gossiping and spreading rumors can damage a person's reputation and should be avoided when engaging in small talk. While it might seem harmless, gossip can quickly become malicious, and the last thing you want to do is hurt someone's feelings or reputation with idle words. Instead, stick to lighter topics like current events, films, books, and music.

Celebrity Gossip

Celebrity gossip is one of the more common topics that can be brought up during small talk. But in conversations with strangers, gossip about celebrities should be avoided. Celebrity gossip can often become a slippery slope of controversial and unwanted discussions. Often people unfamiliar with each other have wildly different opinions about the same celebrity or situation, which could lead to a heated and ugly altercation.

For example, suppose you're talking to someone who's a big fan of Ronaldo, and you bring up a recent controversy surrounding him. In that case, your small talk could quickly turn into an argument.

Some celebrities are famous with Gen-Zers and may not be well-known to older generations, so gossiping about them could lead to confusion and misunderstandings.

Furthermore, there is the potential for different cultural backgrounds and opinions that might not be considered when discussing celebrity gossip with someone you don't know. Celebrities are people too, and negatively talking about them can be seen as disrespectful.

These are some topics generally best avoided when engaging in small talk. When discussing specific topics, everyone has different boundaries and comfort levels, so adjust your conversation accordingly. A little courtesy can go a long way in ensuring discussions remain lighthearted and pleasant. With the right attitude, you can make small talk an enjoyable experience for both parties.

Non-Verbal Ways to Avoid Uncomfortable Conversation

Sometimes it is difficult to steer the conversation away from an uncomfortable topic. However, you can opt for a few non-verbal ways to minimize the awkwardness without directly addressing it.

Change Body Posture

When a conversation makes you uncomfortable, it can be helpful to subtly shift away from the other person. Turn your body at an angle or cross your arms, which creates a visual barrier without you having to say anything or cut the conversation off.

Your facial expression can be a powerful indicator that you're not interested in where the conversation is going. Make a subtle, neutral face and avoid responding with emotions or opinions.

Equally, look for cues that the other person is uncomfortable. Suppose they're shifting away from you, crossing their arms, or frequently looking away. In that case, it's a sign they are uninterested in the conversation. Pay attention to their body language and adjust accordingly.

Take the initiative to steer the conversation in a different direction if you're uncomfortable. Ask the person questions that will lead to more positive topics. You can create an atmosphere of comfort and openness to build a rapport with the other person.

Tone of Voice

The tone of your voice is essential for avoiding unpleasant conversations. Speak soothingly and pleasantly to help create a more relaxed atmosphere. Avoid loud or aggressive tones, as these can make the conversation awkward and distract people from continuing the conversation. Keep your volume moderate, and remember to smile when you talk, as smiling can make a huge difference. Always be courteous and respectful when talking to someone, even if you are not particularly familiar with them or don't agree with their opinions. Being polite helps ensure the conversation remains pleasant and is less likely to lead to difficulties.

Mentally Prepare Comebacks

When someone is engaging in a topic that makes you uncomfortable, it can be helpful to have a few responses up your sleeve that is polite but also assertive. Instead of saying, "I don't want to talk about that," you could say, "I'd rather not talk about this right now. Could I ask you about something else?" Asking to talk about something else opens the door to more interesting discussion topics.

Although it can be hard to come up with the perfect retort on the spot, if you practice a few go-to responses beforehand, you'll be more prepared to pause the conversation and redirect it to something that works for you.

In conclusion, navigating through small talk and bypassing uncomfortable conversations is key to succeeding in social settings. With the right attitude and a bit of mental preparation, you can make small talk an enjoyable and rewarding experience. Remember, everyone has different boundaries for topics, as do you, so adjust your conversation accordingly. Something that might be completely uninteresting to you can be a source of great fascination for someone else, so always stay mindful when talking to strangers.

Chapter 6: Strike Up a Conversation with Literally Anyone

When you see someone you'd like to speak with, whether at a party, conference, or simply out and about, stop and introduce yourself. It could be someone you've admired for a long time, a potential client for your business, or someone you find attractive.

You attempt to formulate the ideal opening remark for a conversation. Still, before you can, the other person has moved on or begun a new discussion, and the opportunity has passed.

The way you start a conversation sets the tone.
https://www.pexels.com/photo/photo-of-people-talking-to-each-other-3182765/

You can initiate a conversation with anyone anytime and in any circumstance. The only trick is to say something that engages the other person.

In light of this, it should be clear that most complaints, political commentary (unless you truly understand the listener's politics), and anything else that could be construed as offensive is strictly prohibited.

Below are some tips for initiating a conversation with anyone. You may even start talking immediately and transition rapidly from being strangers to close friends. At the very least, you could obtain contact information you can use later.

How to Initiate a Conversation

Starting the Process

Create the setting first. For instance, if you attended a business conference held in a large hotel and spent the morning attentively listening to a series of presentations and round-table discussions, you may not have had the opportunity to meet the other attendees.

Now that it's lunchtime, you have the chance to socialize. These tips apply even if you haven't started networking.

Avoid Boring Subjects

Always avoid boring subjects. For instance, you ask, "How's the weather?" or "How about [insert regional sports team name]?" Unless it is headline news, these can be ineffective cheesy pick-up lines.

Since every circumstance is unique, you must be able to generate a unique conversation starter.

Collecting Data

Posing a question or series of questions to a stranger initiates a conversation effectively. Depending on the situation, you could ask about the weather, lunch, or shared professional responsibility. You could ask, "Do you know if the company's president will speak at the opening event?"

As you take in their response, consider follow-up questions or comments you can make to keep the conversation going.

Compliment the Stranger

Complimenting a stranger is another way to start a conversation. Consider this instance: "I like your briefcase."

To continue the conversation, ask follow-up questions, such as where the briefcase was purchased and if it is available in other colors.

Bring Up a Common Subject

Utilize your environment as a conversation starter. Ask the person seated next to you at a workshop or conference what they thought of the event. If you are ordering lunch, let the person behind you know your favorite dish.

Here's another example, "Do you work here? Yesterday, I saw your vehicle parked next to mine."

Identify Yourself

Introductions are an easy way to begin a conversation with someone. It is particularly effective when no other obvious conversation starters are available. For instance, "Hello, my name is Andrew. I'm new to the area and wanted to introduce myself to everyone in the division."

Most likely, the person you're meeting will provide their name and details about their occupation, sparking a conversation.

Pose Wide-ranging Inquiries

Asking open-ended questions is another effective method for initiating a conversation with anyone. This strategy is most effective when you can inquire about another person's participation in a shared event.

Think about this: "I've never attended a workshop as exciting as this one. How about you?"

Typically, the other person will respond with their thoughts or anecdotes about previous conferences they attended, providing you with additional conversational topics.

Keep Up to Date on Current Events

Recent events are great conversation starters. Referring to non-political events is preferable when you and the other individual hold opposing viewpoints. Consider mentioning a nearby festival, a recently published book, or a recently released film. For instance, "Have you heard the Holiday Festival starts the week after Thanksgiving? I always enjoy exploring the decorations."

Offer to Assist

Offering assistance to someone who appears in need is an effective way to initiate a conversation. Depending on the context, you could say, "I could hold onto that box for you if that's okay. Are you a newcomer here?"

Share a Fascinating Fact

This strategy works best when you're in a related environment or situation. This method can be very effective for initiating a conversation with anyone if used correctly. For instance, "Did you know, statistically, riding in an elevator is the safest option?"

Request Their Feedback

Consider asking a total stranger their opinion to spark a conversation. If you are dining out or looking for pens in the office supply closet, this is a good idea. Here is an example of how to employ this strategy: "Which of these highlighters do you prefer? The purple ones are visually appealing, but I typically use these yellow ones."

Get Some Lunch Recommendations

Asking a stranger where they enjoy eating lunch is a good icebreaker. Due to the transient nature of the conversation, this is especially useful in elevators, taxi lines, and public transportation.

For example, "Where is your preferred restaurant? Since I usually work in an office on Fifth Street, I'm unfamiliar with this area."

The stranger will likely recommend their favorite eateries, and they may invite you to join them for lunch.

Speculate on a Trending Video

A viral video is an effective discussion starter. Many individuals spend their free time viewing videos or learning about them from friends or coworkers. Ensure the video you reference is appropriate for your workplace if you employ this strategy. You could ask, "Have you seen the video of the baby sleeping in a frozen yogurt bowl?"

This could spark a conversation about other intriguing video content or popular culture.

Keep It Simple

Occasionally, the most effective way to initiate a conversation is to be direct and honest about what you want or need. For instance, if you are lost, ask for directions.

Indicate if you wish to have lunch with a different individual. Open the conversation with this question, "It's my first day here, and I'm not sure where to eat lunch. Could I please join you?"

Seek Assistance

Ask for help to start a conversation. Depending on the circumstances, you might need to request assistance from a specific individual rather than everyone nearby.

Consider this example: "I have never worked in this office before, so I am unsure how well the copier functions. Can you kindly help me?"

Talk about Shared Interests

In certain circumstances, it might be evident you and a stranger share common ground. Start a conversation with the signals you pick up on.

Example: "You appear to support the local basketball team. Last week, I attended their sporting event. Have you attended any games this year?"

Make a Wise Observation

Commenting on your current situation is another way to initiate a conversation with someone. This strategy is most effective when making a particular point.

For example: "I see you prefer to use your smartphone over a headset."

This remark allows the stranger to express their views on the topic.

Name a Certain Characteristic People Have

Utilize this strategy when you are certain you and the individual share a common trait. One of the most effective ways to establish a connection immediately is to discuss a shared characteristic.

Consider this example: "I observed you signed in with your left hand, and I am also left-handed."

When special traits are involved, most individuals enjoy discussing connections.

Question Them Regarding Their History

Inquiring about someone's background is a professional and amicable way to initiate a conversation.

For instance, "Greetings from the team. Where were you before you came here?"

Ask for Guidance

To initiate a conversation, ask a stranger for advice.

For example: "I am uncertain of the presentation format I should employ. Could you please review it and provide me with some feedback?"

Review a Shared Activity

You could comment on a shared hobby or interest if it is obvious. For instance, you encounter a stranger reading your favorite book in your building's hallway. In this case, say, "When we exited the subway, I noticed you were reading. I completed this book a week ago. Are you enjoying it?"

Make a Joke

You can tell them a joke as an additional method for initiating a conversation with a stranger. The joke must be relevant to your situation with the stranger to be most effective.

For example, you could say, "What could possibly ruin your Friday? Oh... remembering it is *only Thursday* today."

Positive Initiative

Approach the conversation with a positive attitude despite your anxiety. You will gain confidence in your interactions' success and place your trust in others.

It will calm your mind and make you appear much more approachable than if you're anxious. Positivity can be communicated through relaxed body language, a smile, and direct eye contact.

Identify Yourself

Introduce yourself simply, tell them about yourself, and shake their hand to start a conversation. This action is particularly useful if you are out of conversation starter ideas. For example: "I am Mike. I am the marketing manager for [name of company]. How are you doing?"

You will make a strong first impression. Get the other person's name and some personal info to establish a foundation for your conversation.

Don a Peacock Accessory

Wearing a "peacock piece" is another conversation starter. It should be something eye-catching and expressive of your personality, like colorful socks or a tie, which can be appropriate. Expressive clothing or accessories draw attention and spark conversation.

For example, event planners may also offer wearables – achieving the same goal – if you are at a conference. They may request you wear a pin or sticker with your favorite film or sports team logo alongside your nametag. This can serve as a conversation starter with other attendees.

Mention a Common Friend

"Have you worked with Roger before? I've collaborated with him on several projects." By mentioning a shared acquaintance, you demonstrate you are part of the listener's larger social network.

Many will begin to recognize you as someone they know or should know. Be careful that they get along with your mutual acquaintance. You don't want to claim to be best friends with someone they're embroiled in a legal battle with.

Comment the Listeners

This strategy is useful when you don't know what to say to a celebrity, a well-known venture capitalist, or a key figure in your industry or organization. It is never considered an insult to suggest, "I appreciate your work" or "I thought your most recent blog post was very insightful."

Avoid flattery and criticize the listener by saying, "I thought your most recent film was much better than last year's." Furthermore, only offer genuine compliments.

Whenever Appropriate, Mention Their Private Data

As the other person reveals more about themselves, make an effort to recall specifics. It could entail addressing them by name, or it could be an excellent way to continue the conversation.

For example, suppose they pause after they mention their significant other. In that case, you could inquire about their partner's occupation or how they met.

Pose a Theoretical Question

These can be excellent conversation starters, but to avoid sounding too random, relate them to a current event or the occasion.

You could say, "I just saw a movie where all laws were suspended for a day. What would you do if there were no regulations for a day?"

Ask about Their Families, Pets, and Hobbies

People enjoy discussing personally significant topics. If you know your boss enjoys sailing, inquiring about his most recent voyage is a great conversation starter.

Continue Your Conversation

Icebreakers, for example, will only get you far in a conversation. The key is actively engaging your conversation partner and adapting your response to their remarks to make them feel at ease.

Strategies for Starting Conversations and Moving Beyond Small Talk

The following are strategies for initiating conversation with others:

Ask Many Questions

Make an effort to approach conversations with curiosity and an open mind. Asking personal and professional questions can assist you in achieving this objective.

"What were your thoughts on the keynote speaker?"

"What have been the highlights of your training so far?"

"What prompted you to sign up for this conference?"

All these questions are open-ended, indicating your conversation partner must consider the question and provide additional information instead of a simple yes or no response. Consequently, you will have more opportunities to continue the conversation and ask questions.

Search for Receptive Side Doors

A "conversational side door" is an opportunity to deviate from a topic due to something your conversation partner has said. As you listen, be attentive to statements that may have a negative context.

For Instance:

Speaker one: "I've been looking forward to this keynote speech for a while now. When I heard them speak in Phoenix lady year, I was very impressed by their ideas."

You: "I, too, am eagerly anticipating their presentation. Why did you visit Phoenix last year? I've never been there."

In this instance, your conversation partner made a passing remark. However, by being attentive and inquisitive, you uncovered a conversational side door about Phoenix. You can now discuss the city and see where that conversation leads.

Concentrate on Common Interests

If you wish to diverge from strictly business-related topics, find additional topics to discuss. You could share similar tastes in fashion, a passion for high-quality notebooks, or an interest in playing an instrument.

You could share a friend. They may have attended the same university as your preferred teammate, allowing you to discuss them, the university they both attended, and the other team members. Many fascinating topics can be discussed simply by bringing up a common connection.

Although these connections have nothing to do with work, they help you get to know each other better and pave the way for a long-term partnership. If you and a prospective client are golf enthusiasts, you can schedule business meetings while taking practice swings at a driving range.

Learn the Skill of Listening

The most important thing you can do during a conversation is to be present and attentive. This suggests:

Maintaining Eye Contact

Although you are not required to look directly into their eyes, you should devote sufficient time to remembering their eye color. This demonstrates engagement and interest.

Anticipating a Pause before Making Inquiries

Clarification requests are an excellent way to keep a conversation moving. Still, you shouldn't do so at the expense of the other person's current thought process or changing the subject. Allow the conversation to flow naturally.

Pay Attention to Nonverbal Cues

Frequently, communication relies on what is not said. You are responsible for recognizing and responding appropriately if they make a subtle gesture suggesting they wish to end the conversation.

Listen before Talking

Without experience, learning how to initiate a conversation with someone can be difficult. You fear speaking awkwardly or being forced to sit in silence, but by focusing on the other individual, you can alleviate this pressure.

The most common misconception about initiating conversations with others is that you must speak continuously. However, communication with another individual is not required to be extensive. You risk coming across as arrogant or self-absorbed if you ramble on for too long.

After establishing rapport, asking a few well-placed questions will generate a more fruitful discussion than if you were to only talk about yourself.

Approach people with genuine interest and curiosity. These abilities will help you overcome shyness. The more you practice, your reputation as an expert conversationalist will grow.

What Makes a Good Conversation?

A conversation consists of numerous elements. Listed below are several factors to prevent awkward silences:

Engaged Hearing

Active listening involves paying close attention to what someone is saying. Occasionally, participants in a conversation listen to react rather than to understand what the person is saying.

If you use this crucial listening skill, your conversation partner will notice you are attentively listening. It displays emotional intelligence. Furthermore, you will likely recall more of the conversation.

Repeating what you just heard to the speaker improves active listening skills by requiring you to speak less and listen more.

Asking and Responding to Inquiries

Another way to demonstrate you are a good listener is by asking questions.

Responding to another person's statement, you can extend the conversation by asking questions. Alternatively, you can inquire about something you are unsure of or wish to learn more about.

Again, this demonstrates to the other individual that you are genuinely interested in what they are saying.

Discovering Shared Interests and Characteristics

Listen carefully during conversations to identify shared experiences. Keep the conversation flowing by bringing up mutual interests, which will provide you with suitable topics to discuss.

Finding shared interests will help you initiate a conversation and make it more productive. This is essential for maintaining a conversation's flow.

Setting a Goal for the Discussion

Before beginning a conversation, it is always a good idea to have a plan in mind, whether you've run into a colleague at the store or are attending a networking event.

If you have a clear purpose, the conversation will have direction and won't feel awkward or uncomfortable.

If you see the conversation is lagging, introduce a new topic by referencing the conversation's objective.

How to Have a Successful Conversation

Still struggling to hold a conversation? Here are some tips for engaging in fruitful conversations in formal and informal settings:

Ask Numerous Questions

Allow the other individual to respond and take the initiative. Obviously, you do not want them to feel like they are being interrogated.

Avoid Contentious Issues

Always be aware of your surroundings and the people you are speaking with. Avoid discussing sensitive or controversial topics; this could pertain to anything, including politics or religion.

Smile

When initiating conversation, a smile can go a long way. Before speaking, smile at your potential conversation partner. A smile demonstrates your approachability and friendliness.

Establish Eye Contact

Maintaining eye contact conveys your interest and participation in a conversation.

If you constantly look around, the other person will assume you are uninterested in what they say or are distracted.

Offer Compliments

A thoughtful gesture, like a kind remark, is never overlooked. When you compliment your conversation partner, they will feel good about themselves. Additionally, it enriches your conversation.

Pay close attention to what they say so you can look for opportunities to compliment them sincerely.

Seek Suggestions or Advice

Seek suggestions or advice if you are unsure how to maintain a conversation. It demonstrates your appreciation and interest in what they are saying.

It is not difficult to talk to anyone about anything at any time. You will confidently become a great conversationalist with focus and a willingness to learn.

Chapter 7: 50 Foolproof Questions to Ask Anyone

Everybody has experienced the sinking sensation in their stomach when we begin an awkward conversation, and it continues awkwardly until the conversation comes to an abrupt halt. Making and maintaining a conversation is challenging because it requires a continuous flow of thoughts and ideas between the participants.

It has been established that starting a conversation is more difficult for people than keeping one going. It could be due to several factors, including low self-esteem, self-consciousness, social anxiety, and a lack of conversational ideas.

There are specific questions that you need to remember that can work in any situation.
https://www.pexels.com/photo/young-diverse-colleagues-working-remotely-together-4049960/

Conversational ideas can be comfortably discussed with one or more people. They are commonly referred to as small talk and can go a long way toward assisting you in having smooth conversations.

There are good small talk topics (weather, work, and food) and bad small talk topics (sex, death, health), which have been adequately addressed in previous chapters.

Before you start a conversation with someone, especially a stranger, make a mental note of everything you want to discuss. A good small talk topic will kickstart your discussion in the right direction, whether you approach them for help, business, fun, or just a chat.

How does small talk get started? Small talk follows a specific pattern where you provide information before asking a question. For example, when you meet someone for the first time, you introduce yourself and then ask for their name. Making small talk follows the same pattern but entails more than just introducing yourself.

You must understand that the information you provide and the questions you ask determine the success of your conversation. As a result, ensure the questions you ask are concise, clear, and error-free. Using questions like these ensures good responses, leading to wonderful conversations.

What Are Foolproof Questions?

A foolproof question is designed and delivered flawlessly, leaving no room for confusion. They are brief, understandable questions to help you achieve your goal of successful communication. They are also known as guaranteed questions.

The following are some characteristics of foolproof questions:

- They never get old, making them useful for conversation in any situation.
- They help you gather useful information that could come in handy when meeting the same person again.
- They are clear, concise, and self-explanatory.
- They can emanate from any topic.
- They are interlinked, implying you can join questions from one topic to another, making a conversation even more interesting.
- They are subtly placed in conversations.

- They will often get you more than a yes or no answer, allowing you to converse properly.
- They are limitless and come up without you having to think too hard.

Why Should You Employ Foolproof Questions?

Before you use foolproof questions in your interactions with people, you must know why it is recommended.

Using Foolproof Questions

1. **Helps you find common ground:** Foolproof questions help you discover the person's likes and dislikes and will ultimately help you build your conversation on common ground.
2. **Helps you in building social skills:** Communication is a social skill, and implementing foolproof questions regularly in conversations will develop this skill, making you better at discussions and, ultimately, communication without having to try too hard.

   It also helps you develop other social skills, such as empathy, active listening, relationship management, etc.
3. **Helps you interact comfortably:** Foolproof questions will make the other person warm up to you, making the conversation easier and ridding you of unnecessary awkwardness.
4. **Puts you in charge of the conversation:** Foolproof questions put you in control as you steer the discussion in the direction you prefer.
5. **Helps you create a bond:** Foolproof questions often quickly extract valuable information from people, forming a bond between you.

How to Use Foolproof Questions

Using foolproof questions requires a few conditions to be put in place to reap its maximum output.

1. **Read the room:** Before using foolproof questions in your conversations, ensure you have thoroughly read and understood the environment. Do not approach someone having a bad day with a big smile. Address the person by their mood, and listen to what they say. Correct assessment will greatly assist you in determining your questions.

2. **Your questions must be relatable:** When asking foolproof questions, they must be as relatable to the other person as possible. It might appear challenging initially, but asking questions based on how you met the person is a good place to begin.

   Inquire about sports with someone you met at a game. If you meet someone in a library, ask about their favorite authors. Ask someone you meet at an art exhibition about their inspirations in art and who they consider their role models. Conversations will feel more natural if you begin with themes already familiar to both parties.

3. **Employ active listening:** It is not enough to merely ask questions; you must also listen carefully to what they say. It is necessary to ask questions to acquire answers, but if you are not paying attention, the answers are pointless. It is much simpler to carry on a conversation if you actively listen because it helps prepare your next comment or inquiry.

4. **Provide information:** When the questions you've asked are answered, ask another. However, conversation involves both parties sharing information. The person you are conversing with will have questions for you. Be careful to respond appropriately, providing sufficient information without making the conversation too intimate by giving too much information initially.

5. **Be true to yourself:** When conversing with someone, it is best not to exaggerate aspects of who you are. You should avoid putting on an accent, polish your stories, or modify anything

about yourself to please the other person. Showing up in your natural state will boost the likelihood of your success.

50 Practical Foolproof Questions That Work

Foolproof questions never get old. As a result, we've compiled a list of 50 questions divided into different categories so you can have more productive conversations.

Category A: Weather

Talking about the weather with strangers is a tried and true method for breaking the ice and starting a great conversation. By introducing new topics of interest, foolproof questions make it even more enjoyable. The following are some examples of weather-related questions:

1. It's a lovely day, with the sun out like this. What do you think?
2. It's really cold. Are you sure you are okay standing out here in the open?
3. The snow has been coming down a lot lately. Will the (party, service, meeting, etc.) be held?
4. Do you trust the weather forecast?
5. What is your favorite weather?

If you decide to begin a conversation about the weather, keep it brief because people will quickly become bored if all you do is talk about the weather.

Category B: Arts and Entertainment

Almost everyone lights up when a movie, novel, poem, or other art piece is mentioned. Use this advantage, especially if you see them carrying something that suggests their interest in it. You can accomplish this with the following questions:

6. I just (saw/read/listened) to this (movie/book/music) yesterday. Did you like it? Have you...?
7. You have seen the new movie, haven't you? What did you think about it?
8. I love reading (name of author) books; they are delightful. I take it that you like them too?

9. (Musician's name) makes awesome music. What is your favorite track/album?

10. Are you reading any good books right now? I'd love some recommendations.

11. What was the last movie you saw?

Even if your preferences differ, listen to the other person's words without prejudice. You may just grow to appreciate what they appreciate; even if you do not, you will have learned something.

Category C: Travel

When you're on vacation, you'll be engaged in conversations regarding traveling. You should use these questions extensively because everyone else is also probably taking a vacation.

12. Hi, I'm (name). What's your name?

13. Where are you from?

14. Is this your first time here on vacation? Where else have you been?

15. Are you here alone?

16. You've been to many places. Which is your favorite so far?

17. Which place is top of your bucket list right now?

Remember to share your wishes and views with the other person and see if you are similar.

Category D: Work

These questions are frequently asked on formal occasions and are excellent for starting talks with other professionals from different organizations. The following is a selection of examples of questions suitable for this context:

18. How did you rise to where you are now?

19. Would you rather be doing something else other than (job)? What would that be?

20. What does a typical workday look like for you?

21. What are you working on right now?

22. What are your future goals for work?

Category E: Hobbies

It is usually a good idea to ask questions regarding people's hobbies because different questions can be drawn from the topic. Some examples of these questions are as follows:

23. What do you do in your free time?
24. My hobbies are (include hobbies). What are yours?
25. Do you ever think of making money through your hobbies?
26. Show me how it works, will you?

Category F: Family

Another good small talk source is family; there will always be topics to discuss. These are some questions:

27. When and where were you born?
28. Did you have a nickname while growing up? Care to share?
29. Are you still called by your childhood nickname?
30. Do you follow a religion? (If the religion differs from yours, it's best to change the topic)
31. Do you have any family traditions? What are they?
32. Do your parents still live in the house you grew up in?
33. Are there any famous people in your family?

While this is an interesting topic, keep it brief and simple to avoid prying. You don't want to be perceived as nosy by the other person.

Category G: Food

The following are some questions on how food is a fantastic discussion starter and maintainer:

34. Did you enjoy what was served?
35. What is your go-to junk food?
36. What is the most surprising thing you have ever eaten?
37. What would it be if you could eat only one thing for the rest of your life?
38. If you were a meal, what meal would you be?
39. What food would you refuse, even at the cost of death?

Be prepared to laugh at the answers you will receive, as they may surprise you.

Category H: Technology

While technology can be boring to discuss with some people, you will have fun discussing various gadgets with the right people. Some good starter questions are:

40. I can see you're using a (name of gadget). That's cool. Why'd you chosen that one?
41. If you could pick any phone in the world, what would it be?
42. What do you think of the scientific advancements in (health, agriculture, etc.), especially (mention a specific scientific event)
43. iPhone or Android?
44. Would you consider being a freelancer in (mention a tech field, e.g., cyber security, web design, etc.)?

Conversations like these can quickly become rowdy, so know when to move on.

Category I: Sports

Everyone has an affinity for sports, and it is up to you to figure out what that affinity is and craft your foolproof questions accordingly. The following are some sports questions that should be considered:

45. What sports do you play? Which ones do you follow?
46. Did you ever play sports with your school team?
47. Who is your favorite professional athlete right now? Why?
48. Which team are you rooting for in the game?
49. How often do you play?
50. Can I join your team?

Things to Note When Using Foolproof Questions

While you may need foolproof questions to up your conversation game, you must first understand how they work to apply them correctly.

1. **You don't have to start your conversation with a foolproof question:** If you are not confident you will do well by starting with a surefire question, use something else. You can begin with an introduction, a compliment, or a combination.

It is not always necessary to begin with a question. For example, if you are at a gathering and notice someone, you can start talking with an introduction even if you have never met the person. Compliment their clothing or their hairstyle. After that, you can inquire about their well-being and who they came with. You'll notice that you're gradually easing into small talk and can start asking questions.

2. **Remember, the number of foolproof questions is infinite:** the questions listed above guide how they are formed and what they do. As a result, you can always change the questions or create your own. All you have to do is watch the person you want to talk to, figure out something about them, and go in.

   When creating your questions, ensure they are in your area of expertise. When you know nothing about space, could you not ask questions about it?

   If you must ask questions not in your area of expertise, inform the person that you are inexperienced. Make sure you don't embarrass yourself.

3. **Avoid bad small talk topics entirely:** This rule is especially important when meeting new people or distant acquaintances. Small talk topics such as sex, death, and politics could spark an argument or cause tension between you.

   If the conversation does get there, make an effort to get it out as soon as possible. Move on after politely expressing yourself on the subject.

4. **Be confident in yourself:** When a scared person asks the best foolproof questions, they may appear pathetic. Your confidence heavily influences the delivery of your questions. As a result, before engaging in conversation, instill confidence in yourself.

   Remember, the people you're talking to are probably shy and nervous, so it's perfectly normal to be scared.

5. **Be charming:** Foolproof questions work best when delivered as a gentleman and a lady. Take extra care to be decent and polite when conversing and asking questions, as this will endear you to people's hearts.

6. **Do not lose sight of the aim of the conversation:** Depending on who you're speaking to and why you should modify the amount of time you spend making small talk.

   If you are hanging out with a buddy or acquaintance, it is absolutely appropriate to talk to them for as long as you wish. Before bringing up your topic of interest in a chat with someone for information, keep your questions brief, straightforward, and respectful.

   You should stick to this since, for most individuals, inquiring about their well-being and where they live is all the small talk they require before getting bored, especially if they know you're pursuing something.

7. **Be sincere:** Sincerity in conversation cannot be overstated; it can be a game changer when used correctly. As a result, when making small talk, strive to be truthful and honest. It makes a world of difference.

8. **Suggest a "next time:"** When you have a pleasant discussion with someone, you should recommend continuing the discussion the next time you encounter that person. You will have a better chance of acquiring a new acquaintance and establishing a connection if you make this one-of-a-kind action.

9. **Build on your questions:** If you realize that asking foolproof questions is your best bet for a smooth conversation, expand on it. Building in this sense does not mean inventing new ways to ask the same questions; it means formulating new questions based on previous conversations with that person. You can't always ask the same questions when you meet with someone. Learn about the person's interests and diversify your questions to elicit more information about their likes and dislikes. This line of questioning requires a good memory to remember important details about the person.

Foolproof questions are easy and practical questions that almost anyone can implement. They remain the cheat code you need to engage in meaningful, intelligent small talk. These questions can sometimes seem quite complicated, but they're not. You must know how and where to use them, and you'll be fine.

Always remind yourself that conversations are easy and do not require much effort. You can strike up a conversation on any topic depending on the other participant.

Foolproof questions help build and develop your social skills, they are not limited to the ones listed above, and you can have fun making yours. They can be tweaked to your advantage, helping you effectively control the conversation.

Remember, appearance and approach matter when asking your questions. Always be decent, polite, and sincere while conversing with anyone.

Practice these questions, so you can get the hang of it, and hold on to the practical guides stated here, and you will see results in no time.

Chapter 8: Eye Contact and Body Language Hacks

Although engaging in small talk and asking foolproof questions can start a conversation that will go a long way, there is more to fostering a deeper connection with the other person. You must practice making eye contact and adequately utilizing your body language to establish common grounds for a good connection. Let's learn more about eye contact and body language and use them to your benefit.

Body language plays an important role in making people feel comfortable around you during conversations.
https://www.pexels.com/photo/happy-multiethnic-friends-sitting-in-park-3776808/

The Eyes

Since eyes reveal much about a person's feelings, they are typically referred to as the path leading to the soul. Observing eye movements while conversing is a pivotal step in establishing communication. Typical eye movements include blinking, making eye contact, and avoiding looking into the other person's eyes. Paying attention is the key to understanding someone's body language. Watch for any of the following eye signals:

Eyes Fixed

When a person directly stares into your eyes, it shows their interest in the conversation and is paying attention. However, staring for too long can make the other person feel threatened. In contrast, avoiding eye contact suggests the person feels uncomfortable and might want to end the conversation.

Blinking

While eye blinking is normal, blinking too much or too little can reveal how a person is feeling during the conversation. For example, if the other person flutters too often, they might feel anxious, whereas too little blinking is associated with hiding feelings. Like a professional poker player, people who blink less consciously control their blinking.

Pupil Size

Just like varying light intensity affects pupil size, changing emotions can induce pupil contraction or dilation. The most notable effects of emotions on pupil size are noted when a person gazes at someone or hears shocking news.

Facial Expressions

Consider for a moment how much a person can say via expression. Smiling can convey approval or joy. A frown can represent approbation or satisfaction. Our genuine emotions about a situation can sometimes be read from our facial expressions. Although you claim to be in good health, some might not believe you based on your facial expression.

A few instances of emotions conveyed through facial expressions are as follows:

- Happiness
- Sadness
- Anger
- Surprise
- Disgust
- Fear
- Confusion
- Excitement
- Desire
- Contempt

Even our level of trust or belief in someone's words can be inferred from the expression on their face.

Psychology research has produced numerous fascinating results regarding body language. According to one study, the least unreliable facial expressions were a smile and an eyebrow raise. According to the experts, this look exudes friendliness and assurance. One of the most widely recognized aspects of body language is facial expression. Around the world, similar gestures show happiness, grief, anger, and fear.

According to research by Paul Ekman, a range of facial expressions associated with specific emotions, such as joy, anger, fear, surprise, and sadness, have been determined to be universal. According to research, we even form assumptions about someone's intelligence based on facial expressions.

According to another study, people were more likely to be thought of as intelligent when their faces were smaller and their noses more pronounced. Additionally, those with happy, smiling faces were perceived to be brighter than those with angry faces.

Posture

- Maintaining a straight posture while standing or sitting can show assurance and focus.
- Slouching can be a sign of insecurity or disinterest.
- You can demonstrate you are involved in the conversation and interested in what the other person says by leaning slightly in their direction.

- Crossing your arms over your chest could indicate a closed-off or defensive stance.
- Smiling can convey warmth, enjoyment, and approachability in facial expressions.
- A scowl or frown may express displeasure, disapproval, or negativity.
- You can express surprise or demonstrate you're listening and paying attention by raising your eyebrows.
- You can follow along with and concur with what the other person is saying by nodding your head.
- Nodding your head can convey agreement or understanding.
- Head shaking can be a sign of disagreement or perplexity.
- You can highlight a point or express more information by pointing or making hand gestures.
- Honesty and openness can be conveyed by open hand movements. In contrast, hostility and defensiveness can be through closed or clenched fists.

Proximity

- Being too close to someone when standing or sitting can be intimidating or invade their personal space.
- It may be challenging to engage in meaningful conversation or project a feeling of separation when standing or sitting too far away.
- Establishing a comfortable and trustworthy relationship can be facilitated by maintaining an acceptable distance, sometimes known as "personal space.'

The Mouth

When interpreting body language, always pay attention to the mouth gestures and the person's attitude while conversing. For example, persistently biting their lower lip shows they are suffering from anxiety, grief, or insecurity.

- Someone coughing during the conversation and covering the mouth can be taken as a polite gesture. However, coughing

while communicating could also mean the other person disagrees and hides their anger.
- Although smiling is one of the best body language signals, it can be taken up in various ways.
- A grin can be sincere or a way to convey cynicism, sarcasm, or fake delight.

When reading body language, always pay attention to the mouth and lip gestures shared below:
- Clenched lips are associated with suspicion or disapproval.
- When you see someone biting their lips, it means they are feeling anxious, worried, or stressed out due to a life challenge. Clenched lips are associated with suspicion or disapproval.
- While people cover their mouths when yawning or coughing, some may cover their mouths when concealing emotional responses like grinning after hearing something hilarious or smirking.
- If someone has a raised or slightly tilted mouth, they may feel excited and optimistic while conversing. Conversely, if their mouth and face are lowered during the conversation, they may be upset about an issue, feel grief, or find the communication displeasing.

Making Gestures

Gestures are the simplest form of body language expressions used to communicate and express emotions. Some common hand gestures include waving at someone, pointing a finger, and using fingers to denote numerical values.

Across different cultures and regions, hand gestures have been used for ages and carry meaning. However, the importance of similar hand gestures is perceived differently in other countries. For example, a thumbs-up in the US is seen as a gesture of approval and appreciation. In contrast, countries like West Africa, Iran, and Afghanistan consider the thumbs-up an *insult*.

Here are some basic hand motions and their meanings:
- A person clenching their fists shows they are enraged by something or are fearful of their surroundings.

- While thumbs up are associated with encouragement and support, a thumbs-down is made when someone wants to show their displeasure.
- The okay sign is typically made by joining the thumb and index fingertips while the remaining three fingers stay extended. However, this sign is perceived as a negative and crude gesture in several South American countries.
- In many countries, the victory or V sign denotes success or peace if the palm is facing the intended audience. On the contrary, flipping the V sign is linked to derogatory remarks.

Arms and Legs

Additionally, the legs and arms can communicate non-verbally. Arms crossed might be a sign of defensiveness. Crossing the legs away from another person can signify disliking or unease with that person.

Keeping the arms close to the body could be a tactic to reduce yourself or avoid attention, while widely spreading the arms is an attempt to seem bigger or more in charge.

Consider some of the following cues that the arms and legs send when interpreting body language:

- Crossed arms can be a sign of defensiveness, self-preservation, or closed-off-ness.
- Standing with the hands on the hips can either show that a person is prepared and in control, or it could be interpreted as hostility.
- A person who clasps their hands behind their back may be experiencing boredom, anxiety, or even anger.
- Fingers tapping quickly or fidgeting suggest boredom, impatience, or frustration.
- Legs crossed can signify that someone feels isolated or needs privacy.

Posture

Body language can include vital cues from how your body position is held.

The term "posture" describes how we hold our bodies and a person's entire physical appearance.

A person's posture can reveal a lot about their feelings and cues about their personality. For instance, they are assertive, receptive, or subservient.

For instance, sitting up straight can show that someone is focused and paying attention to what is happening. Conversely, hunching forward when seated can suggest a person is bored or uninterested.

Pay attention to some indications a person's posture provides when attempting to understand body language.

Maintaining an open posture entails leaving the body's trunk exposed. Postures like this convey friendliness, receptivity, and readiness.

Closed posture includes concealing the body's trunk, frequently hunching forward, and maintaining crossed arms and legs. This posture usually signals anxiousness, animosity, and unfriendliness.

Have you ever encountered the phrase "needing personal space? Have you ever felt uneasy when someone approaches you a little too closely?

Anthropologist Edward T. Hall first used the term "proxemics" to describe how far apart people are when interacting. The physical space between people can convey as much nonverbal information as body language and facial expressions.

Hall outlined four levels of social distance that can exist in various contexts.

6 to 18 Inches at Close Range

This degree of physical separation frequently denotes a more intimate connection or higher level of familiarity between people. It typically happens during close physical contact, including embracing, speaking, or caressing.

Individual Range: 1.5 to 4 Feet

This physical separation typically occurs between relatives or close friends. The degree of closeness in a relationship can be determined by how closely two individuals stand to one another while conversing.

4 to 12 Feet is the Social Distance

This degree of physical separation is frequently employed with acquaintances.

You may feel more at ease interacting up close with someone you know reasonably well, such as a coworker you see frequently.

A distance of 10 to 12 feet may feel more comfortable when you don't know the other person well, like with a postal delivery driver you only see once a month.

12 to 25 Feet in Public

In public speaking contexts, this level of physical separation is frequently used. These instances include speaking in front of a classroom of pupils or delivering a presentation at work.

Cultures differ regarding how much personal space people need to feel at ease, so it is important to consider these aspects.

One frequently mentioned example is the distinction between individuals from Latin and North American cultures. While North Americans need more extended personal space when interacting with others, people from Latin countries typically feel more at ease standing closer together.

The Significance of Non-Verbal Communication

In social interactions, body language has many different functions. It can make the following things easier:

Gaining someone's trust can be accomplished through making eye contact, nodding your head in agreement while being listened to, or even unintentionally copying their body language.

Making a point clear: Your message will be conveyed differently depending on your voice tone, body language, how much space you take up, and how you interact with the audience.

Truths coming out: We can infer someone is hiding information or not being completely honest about their feelings when their body language doesn't match what they're saying.

Focusing on your requirements: Your body language can communicate much about your emotional state. For instance, do you have a slouched position, or are your lips pursed or jaw clenched? It could indicate that something about your surroundings is setting you off. Your body could be letting you know you're stressed, unsafe, or experiencing any number of other feelings.

How to Communicate More Effectively without Speaking

Being attentive is the first step in enhancing your nonverbal communication. See if you can observe the physical cues of others in addition to your own.

You could tend to glance at the ground when someone tells you a story. Instead, make eye contact and crack a small smile to demonstrate you are open and engaged in the conversation.

Finding balance is the key to effective body language. For instance, grasping someone's hand relatively forcefully before a job interview can convey professionalism. However, if you grab it too firmly, it could hurt or annoy the other person. Always keep in mind how others may feel.

Continue to improve your emotional intelligence. It is frequently simpler to detect how others receive you the more in touch you are with your feelings. When someone is open and responsive, or, on the other hand, if they are closed-off and need some space, you'll be able to tell.

People can use their body language to feel a specific way. For instance, studies have shown that those with better self-esteem and happier moods maintained a more upright seated posture than those with slumped postures while under stress.

Of course, a whole image is frequently painted by verbal and nonverbal communication and the environment of a situation.

What nonverbal cues are appropriate varies depending on the situation; there is no one-size-fits-all answer. But if you remain attentive and show respect, you'll be well on your way to learning how to read body language.

Eye Contact and Body Language Hacks

- **Maintaining eye contact** can be particularly crucial in formal or professional contexts as it helps project confidence and sincerity. Keep eye contact with the other person for around 60% of the talk, occasionally breaking eye contact to demonstrate you are listening rather than simply staring at them intently.

- **Use positive facial expressions** to convey interest and engagement in the conversation. This includes smiling, nodding, and using other positive facial expressions.
- **Maintain open body language**: Avoid clenching your hands or crossing your legs tightly, which can suggest a closed-off or defensive position. Keep your arms uncrossed. Instead, make an effort to maintain a friendly and open body.
- **Be mindful of your posture.** Sit or stand up straight to project assurance and focus. You can demonstrate your participation in the conversation by angling your body slightly in their direction.
- **Mirror the other person's body language**: As was already mentioned, imitating the eye contact and body language of the person you are speaking to can assist in building rapport. However, ensure you don't overdo it and only do it subtly.
- **Practice in front of a mirror**: Practicing in front of a mirror is a quick approach to improving your eye contact and body language awareness. It helps you understand how other people perceive your nonverbal clues, and you can spot bad habits or mannerisms that you may want to concentrate on changing.
- **Ask for comments**: Getting feedback from others is another method to enhance your use of eye contact and body language. Feedback will help you understand how people interpret your nonverbal messages and help you pinpoint areas that need work.
- **Be mindful of cultural differences**: As was already noted, what one culture deems as proper or successful, body language and eye contact can be interpreted quite differently in another. It's critical to be aware of these variations and modify your communication style as necessary.
- **Pay attention to context:** Body language and eye contact can convey various meanings and messages depending on the situation. The greatest approach to employing eye contact and body language depends on the circumstances and the person you speak with.
- **Keep it natural**: While being mindful of your body language and eye contact is vital, it's also crucial to avoid overthinking it or coming off as stiff or forced. Instead of attempting to control

the other person, communicate with them through eye contact and body language naturally and confidently.

- **Maintaining strong eye contact** helps establish a stronger connection with the other person and enables you to build trust. This is particularly crucial when creating successful relationships that depend on credibility and trust.
- **Use body language to express emotion:** In addition to verbal communication, body language is used to express many emotions, such as joy, rage, or grief. Your communication will be richer and deeper as a result, which will increase its impact.
- **Practice active listening:** These nonverbal clues are crucial to demonstrate you are paying attention to what the other person is saying and using eye contact and body language to express meaning. Suppose you want to convey that you are listening and participating in the conversation. In that case, you can nod your head, make encouraging facial expressions, and maintain acceptable eye contact.
- **Making direct eye contact** with someone is an excellent method to connect with them more profoundly and demonstrate empathy. When attempting to console someone upset or vulnerable, this is crucial.
- **Use your body language to project authority:** When giving a presentation or running a meeting, it is essential to project confidence and authority through your body language. It entails keeping an upright posture while standing or sitting, making strong eye contact, and emphasizing points with gestures.
- **Be mindful of your surroundings:** The context in which eye contact and body language are employed can impact their meaning and relevance. For instance, it could be more challenging to establish strong eye contact or use body language to convey a message in a busy or noisy environment. In these circumstances, it may be essential to communicate using alternative channels, like verbal cues.
- **Establish dominance by maintaining strong eye contact:** In some circumstances, maintaining strong eye contact can be a technique used to demonstrate your authority or establish dominance. However, utilizing eye contact acceptably for the

circumstance is crucial, and be mindful of the possibility that this could come off as aggressive or confrontational.

- **Use positive body language to convey interest:** By leaning in slightly, nodding, and displaying positive facial expressions, you convey you are interested in what the other person is saying and are participating in the conversation. You will establish a stronger rapport.

The information in this chapter will help you maintain positive body language and eye contact, making non-verbal communication much easier and more understandable.

Chapter 9: 5 Everyday Secrets of Social Skills Mastery

If you got this far in the book, you're working hard. You have already taken the first step toward becoming a more confident and socially adept person. You are aware of the importance of these skills and how they can help you in all aspects of life. Now it is time to put that knowledge into practice.

Unlike subjects like math or science, social skills must be learned through experience. Learning to cope with conflict, make friends, and navigate groups is primarily a matter of trial and error when you're young. Children will try different strategies as they figure this out – techniques that don't necessarily work for everyone. Learning to navigate the social world can be a challenging experience. It takes time, patience, and a supportive environment.

Social skills are learned through experience and exposure to different situations.
https://www.pexels.com/photo/group-of-people-drinking-beer-and-having-fun-3009773/

What Are Social Skills?

Social skills are the ability to interact with others positively and productively. These include listening, observing, asking questions, and expressing your feelings and opinions. People focus on everyday interactions when they think about social skills. For instance, you can greet a friend in the hallway, start a conversation with someone at a party, or tell someone how you feel about something. However, social skills have an even broader definition. They are critical for success in school, work, and life. Social skills include more than just the ability to interact with others; they include your ability to manage your emotions, solve problems, and think creatively.

The confidence or motivation to develop social skills can be tricky if you struggle with anxiety. You can significantly improve your ability to navigate everyday situations by taking small steps. The following tips will help you get started on the right path.

1. Start Small

Start small if you're overwhelmed by the thought of developing social skills. Begin by identifying one specific area you want to improve. If you want to talk with someone, look for a friendly-looking person who isn't on their phone or wearing headphones (in other words, pick someone like yourself). Find something in common with them; maybe they have the same book as you.

Practice by talking to a cashier at your local grocery store. You could also compliment or say "thanks" when someone holds the door open for you. Don't worry about being perfect. Focus on doing your best. If you struggle in one area, switch up your approach and experiment with different strategies until you find something that works for you.

If you find initiating a conversation with strangers challenging, you can practice with a friend or family member. Try roleplaying and acting out different scenarios that might arise in conversation with a new person – for example, meeting an attractive stranger or talking to someone at a party.

2. Track Your Progress

As you're practicing social skills, keep track of your progress. Keep a diary or journal, and write down instances where you used the new skill and how it went. Measuring your progress will help keep you motivated, and seeing how much you've improved over time will guide future actions. Consider the following steps to measure progress effectively:

Identify Your Goals

With small talk, your goal can be as simple as making a compliment or more advanced, like an entire conversation. The more detailed your goals, the easier it will be to measure progress. For example, if a goal is to make a conversation last 15 minutes, it's easier to measure progress than if the goal is to make small talk. Once your goals are identified, write them down. This way, you will determine if your efforts are paying off and which areas need more work.

Set a Deadline

As an introvert, it's easy to procrastinate social tasks by saying, "I'll do it later." However, if you push yourself to complete a task by a certain date, it becomes more concrete in your mind and less intimidating. For example, if you want to make small talk with an acquaintance at work but haven't yet done so, set a deadline for one week from today.

Set Milestones

Milestones are intermediate goals to help you get from point A to point B. For example, if you want to go out with more people, set a milestone of having one conversation with someone new each week. If you want to network but don't know where to start:

1. Set a milestone of reaching out to your alum association.
2. Once you've set a milestone, make a note of it on your calendar.
3. Keep track of how you're doing regarding your goal so you can adjust if necessary. For example, if you want to go out with more people but only reach out once a week, set two goals for the following week (instead of one).

Document Your Progress

The best way to hold yourself accountable is by keeping track of how you're doing. It can be as simple as writing down your milestone on a piece of paper and putting it somewhere where you'll frequently see it. Alternatively, keep a spreadsheet with all your networking milestones so you can easily see how far along you are in meeting them. If you've set up an accountability partner or team, share progress reports, so they know what's happening in your life.

Set a reward system for the end of each week if you've met all your milestones. It doesn't have to be anything extravagant, just something that will make you feel good about yourself.

Remember: It's not about how quickly you can reach your milestones; it's about sticking with them for the long haul.

4. Practice Good Manners

Good manners are a crucial part of small talk. How you present yourself, your tone of voice, and how you interact with others can make or break your conversation. Practicing is the best way to get into the habit of good manners. Observe people around you and watch how they interact with one another. When someone near you is talking, pay attention to what they're saying and how they say it. Take note of their tone, body language, facial expressions, and gestures – everything that contributes to their overall image.

An excellent way to practice is by watching a movie or TV show. When the characters are conversing, observe what makes each character unique, and use that information when talking with someone new. When you're at work or school, pay attention to how your teachers and professors interact with students. If they're conversing with someone, figure out what makes them unique. Are they funny? Serious? Relaxed? Businesslike? Notice things that make people different and use those traits when talking with someone new. You'll find that the more you pay attention, the easier it is to talk to people.

5. Behave Like a Social Person

You may have heard the saying, "fake it until you make it," meaning if you act like a confident, successful person, you will eventually catch up with your behavior. The same concept applies to social behavior. If you want to improve your ability to engage in small talk and build connections, practice doing so daily. Here are a few tips to help you better connect with others. Try them and see which ones work best for you; if none do the trick, devise your own way of connecting.

Do It for the Right Reasons

People turn to social skills training for many reasons – to become more confident in their interactions with others or to improve communication skills to land a dream job or relationship. However, if you want to get better at small talk and building connections, your motivation must come from a place of self-interest rather than the need for approval or validation. For example, if your goal is to become more confident when talking with strangers at parties, then focus on how this will benefit you (e.g., making new friends, having fun). If you are motivated to be a great conversationalist and to receive praise from others for this skill, your internal pressure will create anxiety about whether you are being seen as talented when talking with new people.

Give Compliments

If you want to build a strong rapport with someone, complimenting them is one of the best ways. It doesn't mean telling people they look good or they did a good job at something – it means finding specific things about their personality and behavior you admire (e.g., their sense of humor, intelligence, etc.).

Complimenting a colleague on their presentation or commenting on the design of someone's shirt can be an ice-breaker. However, it comes from the heart, not just your mouth. Here are some tips for delivering a sincere compliment:

Pay attention to what you genuinely like about the person so they will feel truly valued and appreciated.

- Don't be obvious. Instead, notice the small things that make someone unique, like their favorite food or hobby, and use these to convey what is special about them and turn it into a memorable experience for you both.
- Don't rely on the same old compliments or responses. Instead, pay attention to personality quirks and praise those instead.

Get Involved

Sitting back and watching the party unfold can be tempting if you avoid social situations. However, it's much more helpful to get involved. Consider finding a social hobby, like volunteering at local charities or learning a new language, to help you engage in small talk regularly. If you find it challenging to start conversations, remember there is at least one topic on which all participants can bond: their mutual interest in the activity.

Host a Brunch

Brunch is an excellent opportunity to socialize with friends, family members, and co-workers. It's also a perfect chance for those who tend toward shyness or awkwardness at parties and small talk. The casual atmosphere of a brunch gathering helps you relax and feel at ease. You

can choose games or activities to get people talking and laughing together. Some ideas for brunch activities include:
Charades
- Pictionary
- Trivia games (with questions about food, cooking, or entertaining)
- Scavenger hunt

Sign Up for a Class

You must expose yourself to different social environments to engage with new people. Taking classes that interest you, like cooking or painting, can help expand your social circle and develop new skills. Start a conversation with someone taking the course; talking is easier when people share common interests. If you don't know anyone taking the same class, consider joining a meet-up group or social club offering similar classes.

Make a Date

If you're more comfortable with one-on-one interactions than large groups, take a page from the book of daters. Instead of going out with your whole crew, go on a date. It's an excellent opportunity to engage in small talk with a new person, and it's even better if you have something in common. You can ask people on dates through social media or in person if you're brave. If you're worried about rejection, don't be. Many people are flattered when someone asks them out.

Keep Up with Current Events

You don't have to be a news junkie to stay in the loop with current events. Most people like talking about what's happening in politics and pop culture, so it's a great way to start a conversation. Ask a question if you're unsure of how to bring up a topic. For example: "What do you think about Trump's latest tweet?" or "Did you watch the Oscars last night?"

If you're more adventurous, share your opinion on a current event. It can be as simple as saying, "I think Trump's tweet was ridiculous." You might not agree with each other, but at least you'll have something to talk about.

6. Practice and Repetition

You must devote time and energy to improving your skills to become a master of small talk. It's more complex than saying a few words and walking away. To perfect your conversational skills, talk to everyone. Everyone has something interesting to say, from the cashier at the grocery store to your boss or co-workers. Here are all the places you can start:

Practice in the Mirror

Face your mirror and practice saying what you want to say out loud (don't look directly at yourself). This exercise helps you become aware of what sounds natural or awkward in your speech patterns and voice tones, which will help you improve your delivery.

Social Media

If you're afraid of starting conversations with strangers, make small talk online before approaching someone in real life. You will get comfortable with the idea of talking to people, and it gives you a better understanding of how to approach someone who doesn't know you. If this sounds weird or too much like online dating, don't worry; you can talk about anything from the weather to an interesting article you read on the Internet.

It takes some of the pressure off and can help you practice conversing in a low-stakes environment. You'll have time to think about your responses thoroughly and not feel pressured to come up with something witty on the spot. Remember, online conversations cannot substitute in-person small talk. This exercise aims to practice talking to people and getting comfortable with it.

Friends and Family

Your friends and family are the perfect people to start practicing with. They know you well, so they can help you navigate awkward moments and offer constructive feedback. It's also easier to talk about current events when you have a shared interest – for instance, if a friend is planning her wedding or your mom is undergoing chemotherapy.

It's harder to talk about personal topics with people who have only known you for a few minutes, so practice by pretending they're not a stranger or are a co-worker. It will force you to think about what you're saying instead of letting your conversation flow needlessly.

Co-Workers

Your co-workers are people you interact with regularly, so they are a great source of conversation. If you have co-workers who aren't your friends, it can be harder to practice with them. They're part of the reason you're nervous in the first place. You don't know if they'll like you or judge you for saying something wrong. So, when practicing with co-workers, don't focus on what they think of you. Instead, focus on being yourself and making conversation easier for you both. For example, if one of your co-workers asks how your weekend was, try not to say "fine" or "good." Think of something specific that happened, so you're talking about something more interesting than merely saying it was good.

If you have trouble coming up with a topic of conversation, consider asking your co-workers about their latest work project or office gossip. It will give you something to talk about and show an interest in what's happening around you. You can also ask your co-workers about their hobbies or how long they've been working there.

Retail Workers

You see many retail workers in your day-to-day life. You could be out shopping with a friend or family and have to wait in line at the cashier, or maybe you're in the store and looking for something particular. Whatever the case, you have an opportunity to make small talk with the cashier.

You can ask the cashier about the weather, the latest news, or even their day. If others are in line with you, start a conversation with them. A simple greeting like, "Hi. How's it going?" is enough to jump-start a conversation. You can also ask them how they like working at the store or their experience there.

If you feel engaging in small talk at the checkout line isn't your strong suit, there are other things you can do to make the experience more enjoyable. One option is to smile and say hello to everyone in line with you. This may seem like a small gesture, but it shows you're friendly and approachable. Also, you can roam around the store and engage in pleasant conversation with the employees or other customers. Initiate the conversation by asking for their thoughts on a product or advice on what to buy.

Strangers

You bump into strangers almost always; in the street, at a store, or in line at the bank. You may feel uncomfortable or awkward because you don't know each other, but you can still make these moments enjoyable. To make a good first impression, smile and say hello to the person. If they respond positively, ask them how their day is going.

If the person walking past looks lost or confused, smile and say, "Do you need help?" or "Do you need directions?" Offering to help will break the ice between strangers and lead to a pleasant conversation. If you're in line at the bank, ask how long they've been waiting or what they think of the new security procedures recently implemented. It will help pass the time and make both parties feel more comfortable with each other. If you need a haircut but don't know where to go, ask another person in the line if they can recommend a place nearby. If a stranger is wearing an interesting piece of jewelry or clothing and you'd like to know where they bought it from, ask them.

Learning how to converse and make small talk is a complex process. It's a skill that takes time to develop and master. While plenty of tips and tricks can help you learn to make small talk, the best way to improve is by doing it. You must put yourself out there and face your fears head-on. The more you practice, the easier it will become. You'll learn to balance talking about yourself with listening to others and how to keep a conversation going so people want to talk with you again. Once you've mastered the art of small talk, socializing becomes much easier. It opens up more opportunities in your personal and professional life. You'll make friends more easily, network at events, and even land better jobs with companies wanting someone who can easily converse with others. The next time you go out, make small talk with the people around you. It doesn't matter if it's at a business event or a bar with friends, get in there and start talking.

Bonus: Small Talk Checklist

Congratulations on finishing all nine chapters of this book and broadening your knowledge of small talk. You may also want more tips or to continue mastering what you've learned (if you haven't already).

You receive a bonus for your determination. All the important points you read in the nine chapters are presented as reminders in this bonus chapter. They are useful, especially when you don't want to forget something. You are provided a checklist in the form of a body of words to help you track your progress in mastering small talk.

In today's world, social skills are essential. It enables you to relate, communicate, and connect with others. Moving through life with a greater sense of fulfillment and forming friendships is necessary. The ability to make small talk will greatly benefit you in your life.

I Know about the Most Important Social Skill

According to the Cambridge dictionary, the meaning of small talk is a "conversation about things that are not important, often between people who do not know each other well."

Small talk is a light and informal conversation involving little more than idle chatter. It is a way for people to exchange pleasantries and get to know each other better in a social setting. It is often used to build rapport and create a friendly atmosphere. Small talk can be about various topics, such as the weather, current events, hobbies, and other general interests. It is not meant to be deep or meaningful but rather a way for people to connect and engage in social interactions.

Everyone on the planet is constantly conversing with someone or another. You can strike up a conversation with a total stranger anywhere, including on planes, at conventions, at parties, in classrooms, in offices, and at other similar gatherings. Small talk can lead to some of the most interesting conversations.

Although small talk is important, you must know that conversing about topics other than small talk is equally important. People with social anxiety, low self-esteem, or timidity often avoid small talk. You cannot communicate effectively without these or other social skills. So, how do you approach someone?

- Overcome your timidity, converse more with people you already know
- Boost your confidence and, in turn, your charisma
- Attend events
- Watch movies and documentaries that focus on the art of speaking
- Read books

If you haven't already, you will realize that small talk is an important and useful social skill, if not the most important.

- Small talk is good conversation starters
- Small talk will help make connections or strengthen ones between you and others. A good relationship is important for personal growth
- It helps build your confidence and your fluency with speeches
- It enables you to develop many more social skills like communication, active listening, and cooperation

I Have Overcome the Difficulty That Comes with Small Talk

It's possible to get the wrong idea about how difficult small talk is just by reading or listening to someone talk about it. However, it can be difficult due to various factors, including low confidence, social anxiety, poor social skills like poor vocal tone, awkward gestures, poor body language, and a lack of social education. Low self-esteem and introversion are also factors.

If you experience difficulties, you should not be concerned because they can be overcome. Although many of these difficulties require you to seek medical help from a mental health professional, the following tips and techniques can help you overcome them. The checklist below outlines the difficulties first, followed by possible solutions. Only select those that apply to you.

- **Low Confidence** - Remind yourself you are as interesting and bold as everyone else.
- **Social Anxiety** - Set a goal to say as much about yourself as the other person does in your next conversation. You can practice with a close friend first. Do this regularly.
- **Low Self-esteem** - Recognize what you are good at, keep doing it, and learn to be assertive.

I'm Introverted, But I Can Pull a Few Tricks with Small Talk

Being an introvert in the real world is difficult. Unlike extroverts, who gain energy from small and large conversations wherever they go, introverts are depleted by them. This is due to various natural causes. One reason is that introverts frequently believe that small talk is too shallow for their introspective souls to engage in.

Forbes listed eight techniques to get through small talk as an introvert. These are the things you should do continuously.

- Seek affirmations like, "I am worthy of happiness and success," or "I stay true to my nature, I live in peace, and I'm excellent at understanding others." These affirmations help reduce anxiety.
- Be kind to yourself, and do things for yourself.
- Ask questions to keep the conversation going and to keep you away from the forefront.
- Add juicy tidbits to your answers. For example, when asked what you did on the weekend, instead of saying you went to see a movie, say, "I went to the cinema to see Titanic. I loved the part where Jack gave up his life for Rose. Have you seen it?"
- Always ask open-ended questions to deepen the conversation when conversing.
- Channel your inner curiosity into figuring out what the other person is like.
- Recognize cues to respond appropriately. Practice this with familiar people.
- Always consider small talk meaningful by practicing being purposeful.

I Can Converse Using Either or All the Best Small Talk Topics

Remember, certain topics are acceptable at any social gathering and will help you make great small talk. Those skilled at small talk will tell you that certain topics make a conversation flow naturally. These are the topics:

- **Family**

You can ask, "How is your family?" Or giving compliments like, "I just saw your husband and the kids. You have an amazing home. What's the secret?"

- **Arts and Entertainment**

If nobody is talking about arts and entertainment, then is anyone talking? However, you should know when to raise this topic.

- **Celebrity Gossip**

This topic would work well at parties, the amusement park, and even at school.

- **Work**

While this is a good conversation starter, you shouldn't talk about your work when you are not looking for new friends.

- **Hobbies**

This is a good one. However, something has to lead to this discussion, like talking about hometowns.

- **Travel**

You can bring this up at airports. You could say, "I see you're going to XYZ. Is this your first time?"

- **Sports**

Not everyone watches sports, so you must be discerning and also not bring it up everywhere.

- **The Weather**

When two Americans meet, it is often said their first discussion is the weather; "Hey friend, I love the weather today and how the wind breezes through me. You feel it, too, right?" This leads them to their more important discussions.

I Know the Worst Small Talk Topics

Some topics are best suited for small talk, while others will ruin your conversations and expose you as a drainer.

- **Appearance**

Everyone loves to be complimented, but be very mindful of talking about someone's appearance.

- **Offensive Jokes**

The keyword here is "offensive." You know the drill.

- **Death**

Never use this topic for your small talk, even at a funeral, especially to the person mourning.

- **Past Relationships**

This topic is also a no-no, like Death. You shouldn't open your conversation with this topic upon meeting someone.

- **Politics and Religion**

Are you looking for a way to end a relationship before it begins? Use this topic.

- **Finances**

Stay away from this starter unless you are at a gathering where finance is discussed or are communicating an issue at the bank.

Some other no-no topics are sex, health, and narrow topics.

I Can Strike Up a Conversation with Anyone

There are several approaches to striking up a conversation with a stranger. Three scenarios will remind you of what was discussed in Chapter 6.

- Are you at a party? Ask open-ended questions like, "Why did you choose that college course" or "How do you see the future?"
- On public transport? You can begin by complimenting someone but not talking about appearance.
- At a sports viewing center? Talk about the last game played by the respective teams.

Remember, striking up a conversation with a stranger depends on the circumstance and the setting. Beyond all of these, there are a few tips to help you strike up a conversation with anyone.

- Don't be pessimistic
- Avoid complaining

- Engage in active listening
- Stay positive
- Always render compliments
- Discuss optimistic topics
- Change the subject if it gets awkward

I Know Some Foolproof Questions to Ask Anyone

You've progressed beyond learning how to initiate a conversation and understanding the dos and don'ts of small talk. Asking people questions, specifically foolproof questions, is the next level of small talk.

A foolproof question is simple yet flawless and certain. Nothing can go wrong. Chapter 7 listed fifty sure questions to make even the most awkward small talk seem easy. Art, weather, sports, family, travel, work, entertainment, food, hobbies, celebrity gossip, hometown, and other related topics generate these questions. Here are a few examples.

- What would you be doing if you weren't working here?
- How did you become a [job title]?
- What would it be if you could only eat one thing for the rest of your life?
- What's the best "hidden gem" around here?
- If you could fly anywhere, where would you go?

I Have Mastered the Art of Eye and Body Language

Asking foolproof questions is an excellent way to start a conversation and take it as far and deep as you want. However, following just one method is insufficient for establishing a good connection. Small talk is more successful when making eye contact and using body language. What we cannot or will not say can be communicated through eye contact and body language.

The following are examples of common eye contact and body language:

- Eye gaze, which shows attention
- Rapid blinking, which could be a sign of distress
- Tightening of the lip to show distaste
- Clenching of fists to show anger or solidarity

- Crossed arms could mean defensive or a way to support the body
- Making facial expressions to show confusion, anger, or happiness

Some of the benefits of these acts are:
- Consistent eye contact makes people focus on the conversation
- Keeping eye contact and projecting body language improves understanding and communication and the trust the other party has in you
- It helps to pick up truths faster, as someone's body language or eye contact has to match what they say
- It is an outlet to show how you feel

Although people often communicate what is true through their body language, you must remember your assumptions might not always be accurate.

I Know and Practice the Secrets to Social Skills Mastery

If you diligently followed all the lists above, you would agree the steps are helpful. You must ask yourself, "What's the way forward?" or "How do I become better at small talk?" The simple answer, the masters' secret in any field in the world, is PRACTICE.

Perfect practice (practice at the right time, in the right place, with the right tools) truly does make perfect. As with many other guides, people who read this book will want to see results immediately, and some will want to see results even before reading the first chapter. Still, no one becomes an expert at anything overnight. Your dedication to practicing the skills will determine whether you become an expert.

What is the significance of daily repetition and constant practice?
- It helps you transfer your skills from the conscious state to the subconscious
- It helps strengthen the connections of learning in the brain
- It increases confidence
- It improves speed
- It leads to mastery

Aside from practicing with people you know, you must go out into the real world and do it. Attempting and starting a conversation with strangers on public transportation, in waiting rooms, stores, or other public places is a good starting point for practicing small talk and social skills and eventually becoming an expert.

You might have heard or said, "I hate small talk," but I bet you now have a different mindset and will gladly engage in small talk anywhere and anytime, improving your social skills as you go along. No book can *make you* start a conversation; that lies with you, and practicing is the best place to start.

Small talk can do wonders. Apart from fostering interpersonal relationships, it also promotes trust and respect. Good small talk will always display your linguistic competence and familiarity with your surroundings and occupation. Small talk is the first step to talking to anyone or building successful relationships with others.

How far have you come?

Consider the small talk checklist below:

Do I actively listen to the other person and show interest in what they say?

Do I ask open-ended questions to keep the conversation flowing?

Do I share personal anecdotes or stories to relate to the topic at hand?

Do I remember and bring up previous conversations or details about the other person?

Do I use appropriate body language, such as making eye contact and smiling?

Do I steer clear of controversial or sensitive topics?

Am I able to keep the conversation light and positive?

Do I keep the conversation balanced, allowing the other person to talk?

Do I use humor and laughter appropriately in the conversation?

Do I make an effort to end the conversation politely and smoothly?

Conclusion

Since there are so many individuals in the world, we must constantly engage in discussions. These conversations frequently begin with small talk, which the Cambridge dictionary defines as *"talking about unessential things, often between people who do not know each other well."*

Small talk is a social skill allowing you to converse with anyone about any topic. Engaging in idle small talk is a great way to create self-assurance and long-lasting relationships. People who struggle with social situations generally find such short talks tedious. The good news is you can get better at it.

The strategies for making small talk discussed in this book are helping introverts have fun in the world. If you are an introvert and want to participate actively in the arts, you can seek affirmation, be kind to yourself, ask open-ended questions, and adjust your attitude toward small talk.

Some of the most interesting and engaging small chat subjects are about families, friends, hobbies, the weather, arts and entertainment, travel, and celebrity gossip. Topics on appearance, obscene jokes, death, politics, religion, and previous relationships should be avoided when engaging in casual conversations.

It is possible to strike up a conversation with a stranger in different ways, and the things you discuss will vary depending on the context. You must understand the topic that corresponds most with your settings.

Pay close attention to the advice provided in this book so that you can be successful. If the conversation feels awkward, you should keep a cheerful attitude, complement the other person, and change the subject. It would be best if you didn't have a negative outlook on life and avoided complaining.

Your small talk game is incomplete when you don't know how to ask questions, especially foolproof questions. A foolproof question is simple, flawless, and certain - nothing can go wrong.

Mastery of eye and body language is another level of small talk. These arts will take your small talk as far as you desire because it is a way to communicate what you cannot say. The examples in this book will improve your communication and boost your trust in others.

Practice is the only way to master any skill, including social skills. Practice makes perfect (practice at the right time, in the right place, with the right tools). It will boost your confidence and improve your skills by transferring them from the conscious to the subconscious.

You probably read this book because you wanted to learn to be more sociable or are curious about psychology. Small talk works wonders; you can talk to anyone using this skill. Use the checklist to hone in and achieve your goals.

Reading alone will not give you the desired outcome. You must actively follow the helpful tips and the active listening guide and consciously practice the outlined practical social skills, like using body language and creating eye contact to overcome fear and social anxiety.

You've read and followed the guidelines of this book, and now you need never fear social gatherings again!

Here's another book by Andy Gardner that you might like

Free Bonus from Andy Gardner

Hi!

My name is Andy Gardner, and first off, I want to THANK YOU for reading my book.

Now you have a chance to join my exclusive email list related to human psychology and self-development so you can get the ebook below for free as well as the potential to get more ebooks for free! Simply click the link below to join.

P.S. Remember that it's 100% free to join the list.

Access your free bonuses here:
https://livetolearn.lpages.co/andy-gardner-how-to-talk-to-anyone-paperback

References

Frost, A. (2019, July 24). The ultimate guide to small talk: Conversation starters, powerful questions, & more. HubSpot. https://blog.hubspot.com/sales/small-talk-guide

Gregory, M. (2020, May 22). 10 chance meetings that changed the world. Mental Floss. https://www.mentalfloss.com/article/624374/chance-meetings-changed-world

Luda, Z. (2018, July 6). 5 Main principles of Small Talk. Language Learning with Preply Blog. https://preply.com/en/blog/5-main-principles-of-small-talk/

Sandstrom, G. M., & Dunn, E. W. (2014). Is efficiency overrated? Minimal social interactions lead to belonging and positive affect. Social Psychological and Personality Science, 5(4), 437–442. https://doi.org/10.1177/1948550613502990

Waber, B., Magnolfi, J., & Lindsay, G. (2014). Workspaces that move people. Harvard Business Review, 92(10), 68–77, 121. https://hbr.org/2014/10/workspaces-that-move-people

Wuench, J. (2021, June 21). Why small talk is anything but small. Forbes. https://www.forbes.com/sites/juliawuench/2021/06/21/why-small-talk-is-anything-but-small/?sh=37d1b97078b0

Cohen, L. (2017, November 15). Social anxiety and small talk: The nuts and bolts of making conversation. National Social Anxiety Center. https://nationalsocialanxietycenter.com/2017/11/15/social-anxiety-small-talk-nuts-bolts-making-conversation/

Denworth, L. (By Lydia Denworth on September 21, 2021). Making eye contact signals a new turn in a conversation. Scientific American.

https://www.scientificamerican.com/article/making-eye-contact-signals-a-new-turn-in-a-conversation/

Murphy, A. (2022, April 26). 20 ways to overcome low self-esteem in 2023. Declutter The Mind. https://declutterthemind.com/blog/how-to-overcome-low-self-esteem/

Okusaga, O. (2022, April 21). How to master small talk as an introvert. Introvertdear.com; Introvert, Dear. https://introvertdear.com/news/how-to-master-small-talk-as-an-introvert/

Social anxiety disorder: Symptoms, tests, causes & treatments. (n.d.). Cleveland Clinic. https://my.clevelandclinic.org/health/diseases/22709-social-anxiety

Social anxiety (social phobia). (n.d.). Nhs.uk. https://www.nhs.uk/mental-health/conditions/social-anxiety/

The basics: Anxiety. (2016, December 15).

Therapists, L. H. G. (2022, April 11). Tips for small talk when you have social anxiety. Sacramento Relationship Therapy | Midtown Therapists | Love Heal Grow Counseling; Love Heal Grow Counseling. https://www.lovehealgrow.com/tips-small-talk-social-anxiety/

Ultimate guide to social skills: The art of Talking to anyone. (2015, October 20). I Will Teach You To Be Rich. https://www.iwillteachyoutoberich.com/guides/ultimate-guide-to-social-skills/

Victor, K. (2017, November 29). Tips for how introverts can make small talk less painful. Linkedin.com. https://www.linkedin.com/pulse/tips-how-introverts-can-make-small-talk-less-painful-kristy-victor/

Website, N. H. S. (n.d.). Raising low self-esteem. Nhs.uk. https://www.nhs.uk/mental-health/self-help/tips-and-support/raise-low-self-esteem/

(N.d.). Blinkist.com. https://www.blinkist.com/magazine/posts/how-to-improve-social-skills

Cuncic, A. (2007, December 9). How to socialize when you have social anxiety disorder. Verywell Mind. https://www.verywellmind.com/talk-people-social-anxiety-disorder-3024390

Macapinlac, M. (2021, December 24). How to make small talk for introverts. Social Confidence Mastery. https://socialconfidencemastery.com/small-talk-for-introverts/

Okusaga, O. (2022, April 21). How to master small talk as an introvert. Introvertdear.com; Introvert, Dear. https://introvertdear.com/news/how-to-master-small-talk-as-an-introvert/

Park, C. (2015, March 30). An introvert's guide to small talk: Eight painless tips. Forbes. https://www.forbes.com/sites/christinapark/2015/03/30/an-introverts-guide-to-small-talk-eight-painless-tips/?sh=57177f5a574a

Venable, M. (2022, May 9). Back to life, back to reality: How to master the art of small talk (in case you forgot). Shondaland. https://www.shondaland.com/live/family/a39929200/how-to-master-the-art-of-small-talk/

Waters, S. (n.d.-a). 8 types of nonverbal communication that can help to improve your speech. Betterup.com. https://www.betterup.com/blog/types-of-nonverbal-communication

Waters, S. (n.d.-b). How to carry a conversation – the art of making connections. Betterup.com. https://www.betterup.com/blog/how-to-carry-a-conversation

Cherry, K. (2019, January 28). 8 Tips for Starting a Conversation. Verywell Mind. https://www.verywellmind.com/how-to-start-a-conversation-4582339

Cuncic, A. (2010, August 5). Small Talk Topics. Verywell Mind. https://www.verywellmind.com/small-talk-topics-3024421

Frost, A. (2019, July 24). The ultimate guide to small talk: Conversation starters, powerful questions, & more. HubSpot. https://blog.hubspot.com/sales/small-talk-guide

Kim. (2020, July 15). Small talk topics and questions keep the conversation going in English. English with Kim. https://englishwithkim.com/small-talk-topics-questions/

Parr, M. (2020, May 26). 10 best small talk topics & conversation starters (+ examples). Language Learning with Preply Blog. https://preply.com/en/blog/small-talk-topics/

(N.d.). Indeed.com. https://ca.indeed.com/career-advice/career-development/small-talk-topics

Cuncic, A. (2010, August 5). Small Talk Topics. Verywell Mind. https://www.verywellmind.com/small-talk-topics-3024421

Topics to avoid in English small talk. (2015, February 15). EF English Live. https://englishlive.ef.com/blog/english-in-the-real-world/topics-avoid-english-small-talk/

(N.d.-c). Inc.com https://www.inc.com/laura-garnett/if-you-hate-small-talk-use-these-20-questions-as-a-conversation-starter-instead.html

Marr, B. (2014, October 27). How to start a conversation with absolutely anyone. Linkedin.com. https://www.linkedin.com/pulse/20141027073838-64875646-how-to-start-a-conversation-with-absolutely-anyone

Perry, E. (n.d.). How to start conversations with strangers: Befriending everyone. Betterup.com. https://www.betterup.com/blog/how-to-start-conversation-with-strangers

Waters, S. (n.d.). How to carry a conversation – the art of making connections. Betterup.com. https://www.betterup.com/blog/how-to-carry-a-conversation?hsLang=en

(N.d.-a). Inc.com. https://www.inc.com/minda-zetlin/10-foolproof-ways-to-start-a-conversation-with-absolutely-anyone.html

(N.d.-b). Indeed.com. https://www.indeed.com/career-advice/career-development/how-to-start-conversation-with-strangers

"11 Foolproof Ways to Start a Conversation With Absolutely Anyone" https://incafrica.com/library/minda-zetlin-10-foolproof-ways-to-start-a-conversation-with-absolutely-anyone

"48 Questions That'll Make Small Talk Easier | The Muse" https://www.themuse.com/amp/advice/48-questions-thatll-make-awkward-small-talk-so-much-easier

"Master Small Talk With These 10 Tips (with Examples) | SuaveWay" https://suaveway.com/blog/master-small-talk/

Bradberry, T. (2019, June 18). 8 great tricks for reading people's body language. Linkedin.com. https://www.linkedin.com/pulse/8-great-tricks-reading-peoples-body-language-dr-travis-bradberry

Fontanella, C. (2022, May 9). 13 body language tips that can make or break your customer service. HubSpot. https://blog.hubspot.com/service/body-language-in-customer-service

Herz, S. (2020, July 16). 10 quick body language hacks from Steve Jobs – and a surgeon – to boost likability and trust. CNBC. https://www.cnbc.com/2020/07/16/steve-jobs-surgeon-body-language-hacks-to-make-you-more-likable-respected-trustworthy.html

Stenstrom, J. (2015, May 22). 11 body language tricks to make you successful in life. Lifehack. https://www.lifehack.org/articles/communication/11-body-language-tricks-make-you-successful-life.html

Thair, R. (2022, August 11). 5 body language hacks to boost your communication. Happiful Magazine. 5 body language hacks to boost your communication (happiful.com)

(N.d.). Inc.com. https://www.inc.com/melanie-curtin/7-body-language-hacks-that-immediately-make-you-more-likable.html

Cooks-Campbell, A. (n.d.). How to improve social skills: 10 tips to be more social. Betterup.com. https://www.betterup.com/blog/how-to-improve-social-skills

Gunnarson, V. (2015, July 10). 10 small talk tips that'll make you forget you ever had to rely on "so, how about that weather?" The Muse. https://www.themuse.com/advice/10-small-talk-tips-thatll-make-you-forget-you-ever-had-to-rely-on-so-how-about-that-weather

Lamothe, C. (2019, July 15). 10 ways to be more social, even if you're an introvert. Healthline. https://www.healthline.com/health/how-to-be-more-social

Morin, A. (2013, December 31). 12 ways to improve social skills and make you sociable anytime - Amy Morin, LCSW. Amy Morin, LCSW. https://amymorinlcsw.com/12-ways-to-improve-social-skills-and-make-you-sociable-anytime/

(N.d.). Indeed.com. https://www.indeed.com/career-advice/career-development/measure-progress

Cherry, K. (2017, July 27). Understanding body language and facial expressions. Verywell Mind. How to Understand Body Language and Facial Expressions (verywellmind.com)

www.ingramcontent.com/pod-product-compliance
Lightning Source LLC
Chambersburg PA
CBHW070337010526
44107CB00004B/538